New Thinking in Design

New Thinking in Design

Conversations on Theory and Practice

C. Thomas Mitchell

VAN NOSTRAND REINHOLD
ITP® A Division of International Thomson Publishing Inc.

New York • Albany • Bonn • Boston • Detroit • London • Madrid • Melbourne
Mexico City • Paris • San Francisco • Singapore • Tokyo • Toronto

Van Nostrand Reinhold Staff
Editor: Jane Degenhardt
Production Editor: Carla Nessler
Production Manager: Mary McCartney
Designer: Jane Tenenbaum

Printed in the United States of America
For more information, contact:

Van Nostrand Reinhold
115 Fifth Avenue
New York, NY 10003

Chapman & Hall
2-6 Boundary Row
London
SE1 8HN
United Kingdom

Thomas Nelson Australia
102 Dodds Street
South Melbourne, 3205
Victoria, Australia

Nelson Canada
1120 Birchmount Road
Scarborough, Ontario
Canada M1K 5G4

Chapman & Hall GmbH
Pappelallee 3
69469 Weinheim
Germany

International Thomson Publishing Asia
221 Henderson Road #05-10
Henderson Building
Singapore 0315

International Thomson Publishing Japan
Hirakawacho Kyowa Building, 3F
2-2-1 Hirakawacho
Chiyoda-ku, 102 Tokyo
Japan

International Thomson Editores
Seneca 53
Col. Polanco
11560 Mexico D.F. Mexico

1 2 3 4 5 6 7 8 9 10 QEB-KP 02 01 00 99 98 97 96

Library of Congress Cataloging-in-Publication Data
Mitchell, C. Thomas.
      New thinking in design : conversations on theory and practice / C.
Thomas Mitchell.
         p. cm.
      Includes bibliographical references and index.
      ISBN 0-442-01733-2
      1. Design—Methodology. 2. Design—History—20th century.
3. Designers—Interviews. I. Title.
NK1520.M58 1996
745.4—dc20   96-33750
                                                        CIP

To Claire

Contents

Preface

For this book I interviewed thirteen leading people from a range of design or design-related fields, each of whom has developed ways of making designing more encompassing and more responsive to those who interact with it. At the beginning of this project I assumed that those to be included had rejected some "bad" aspects of mainstream design practice and that they had each developed more responsive ("good") alternatives. Though this was the basis of my questioning, in almost every case those interviewed rejected this crude formulation, replacing it with their own, much more refined, views.

I am indebted to the participants in this project, each of whom gave freely of his time and insights. *Michael McCoy* explained the theoretical basis of his and his students' much-discussed work, dispelling the widely held belief that product semantics and interpretive design are simply styles. *Daniel Weil,* who has given me a great deal of invaluable advice over the years, took time out from his busy schedule to provide an insight into his highly individual design process. Daniel also kindly allowed me to illustrate this book's cover with images of his remarkable work. *Frank Duffy* spoke with me at what was for him an extremely hectic time. Duffy described his firm's philosophy and work and also addressed the threats being faced by the architectural profession in Britain in the 1990s.

Lucien Kroll is a polemicist as well as an architect and planner. I addressed his work in my first book, *Redefining Designing,* and since that time we have corresponded about the importance of, and difficulties faced in doing, truly collaborative design. In our conversation Kroll gave animated explanations of his firm's work and detailed the various collaborative processes that underpin it. *Clino Trini Castelli* spoke with me from his office in Milan in one of his rare breaks from travel as a design consultant. Castelli detailed his unique design approach, which has focused on the "soft," sensory qualities of design rather than on form. *Edwin Schlossberg* carved out time over his lunch hour to speak with me about his firm's work, the aim of which is to "create conversations" between people and environments.

Kiyoshi Sakashita provided written replies to my questions. In them he explained the ideas behind some of the Japanese design approaches, such as those he employs at Sharp Corporation, which are mentioned but not detailed in the literature. *Donald Norman* spoke to me soon after leaving academia for industry. He has spent most of his career as a leading researcher and writer on psychology and cognitive science but is now directly involved in design issues in his work at Apple Computer. *John Seely Brown* operates in both the business and academic contexts also. In our discussion Brown provided an insight into his work at Xerox Corporation, where advanced concepts of cognition and learning are used to shape the technology of the future.

John Thackara has over the last decade or so established himself as a central figure in design thinking in his roles as a writer, consultant, and *agent provacateur.* He has been extremely helpful to me during this time, providing encouragement and advice on numerous occasions. In our conversation Thackara discussed his own work and shared his insights and views on possible future developments in the design professions. *Larry Keeley* agreed to be interviewed by telephone soon after I began this project, and we had another conversation at Doblin Group's offices in Chicago just before the book's completion. In our discussions, Keeley set out the philosophy of his firm and detailed the nature of *strategic design planning,* the process that Doblin Group uses in its work. *Peter Schwartz* has developed scenario planning, an intriguing approach that is very applicable to design. In our conversation Schwartz not only presented the work of his firm, Global Business Network, but also offered suggestions on how the scenario approach might be adapted for use in design.

I owe an ongoing debt to *John Chris Jones,* whose work has served as a constant inspiration. I return regularly to his writings, which always yield new insights into ways of making design more human. As was the case when I was writing my previous book, Jones served here not only as a muse but also as a critic, pushing me to further develop my work at all times. Though we have frequent discussions, Chris in this case chose to provide written replies to my questions.

Everyone I interviewed has a very full schedule, and I am indebted to their staffs for the help they provided in arranging the interviews, providing images, and following up on my many requests for information. In particular, I would like to thank Julia Wyatt of Pentagram Design Ltd., Mikael Ekström of Facit Office Furniture, Maria Torres of Edwin Schlossberg Inc., Janice Heiler of Xerox PARC, and Michael Tirrell of Doblin Group for the important roles they played in the completion of this book.

I would also like to thank Roy Davis, whom I interviewed on the psychological principles underlying good design, and Alan Hedge, who shared the state of the art in research into health problems in buildings. As this project evolved, it seemed more appropriate to include their work in a future volume on design research than in the present one on design process.

My sincere and heartfelt thanks go out to all of these participants for their kind and generous help with this project. The book literally could not have been realized without them.

Upon taking up my first teaching position, Chris Jones gave me two pieces of advice. The first was not to overcomplicate my teaching, and the second was to befriend the university's reference librarians. I have followed each of these suggestions to my benefit, and in particular have been assisted immeasurably in my research by numerous people at the Indiana University libraries. David Frasier, Jeff Graf, Clay Housholder, B. J. Irvine, and Frank Quinn have been particularly helpful; they are friends as well as colleagues. The librarians have not only responded to my frequent requests for often obscure information, they have also introduced me to a wide variety of new reference sources that have significantly affected and broadened the scope of my research. Jeff Graf in particular has played a critical role in this project, freeing me up to write by his willingness to respond to all of my many requests by return E-mail.

I would also like to acknowledge the help of those who helped keep me focused during the writing of this book. In particular, I would like to thank my wife, Claire, who has now heard the words *the book* daily for almost a decade. She has, throughout this time, remained patient and cheerful, even when I have lacked both qualities. Our dogs, Brutus, Olivia, and Jessica; our Brown County neighbors; and our Bloomington friends have all enriched our lives immeasurably, in large part by serving as reminders of the world that exists beyond "the project." Thanks too to Michael Kane for providing some much-needed perspective at a difficult time and for introducing me to the concept of mindfulness.

Among those with whom I discussed this book as it evolved, and those who offered encouragement and helpful suggestions, I should mention Andrew J. King, an extremely astute historian of design thinking, from Bath, England; Ron Mowat of Syracuse University, a former colleague who brings emerging concepts of all kinds to my attention; Phil Kunze, a design consultant based in Kalamazoo, Michigan, who specializes in the analysis of communication environments; and the members of the Holland, Michigan–based Ambient Design group: Don Shepherd, Susan Monroe, and John Hetrick. Though not addressed in this book, Ambient Design is an emerging concept that promises to be one of the most inclusive and powerful developments in design in the coming years. The collective intelligence and enthusiasm of these people has been a true inspiration.

The concept for this book was suggested by Wendy Lochner, and though it has changed a great deal from the initial idea we discussed, it still owes its origin to her. John Griffin made a number of very helpful suggestions, and Jane Degenhardt played a critical role in its realization, patiently working to resolve last-minute issues and shepherding the book through the publication process. Special mention should be made of the care and attention to detail that Jane and the staff at

Impressions in Madison, Wisconsin, gave to the production of this book—all in the face of my own occasionally unreasonable demands.

One of the thrills and trepidations of writing a book is the anticipation of the reaction it will receive from readers. In his brilliant book *How Buildings Learn,* Stewart Brand addresses the importance of user feedback to authors and following his example, I would like to invite readers who have comments to E-mail me at mitchelc@indiana.edu.

I hope you enjoy the book, and I look forward to hearing from some of you.

Tom Mitchell
Yellowwood Forest, Indiana
Autumn 1995

Introduction

One of the most discussed and contentious issues among designers is the definition of *good design*. It is impossible to reach a consensus of opinion about this, however, as the very nature of the field is constantly debated. A recent compilation of some leading designers' views, for example, yielded the following:

Design is not art. (Rick Vermulen)

Designing is a practical art. (Niels Diffrient)

The designer is in essence an artist. (George Nelson)

A designer is a problem solver. . . . We are not artists. (Henry Wolf)[1]

Given this divergence of opinion on the aims of the designer, the discussion of what is and is not *good* design can quickly become turgid. As design theorist John Thackara, Director of the Netherlands Design Institute, notes, "Defining good or bad design is a vexed—and often tedious—matter: attempts to define good or bad design usually go around in circles."[2]

I agree with Thackara on this but would note further that most attempts to define *good design* focus on aesthetics and pay little meaningful attention to the myriad of different aspects that must be considered to make designs successful in use. Designs can be assessed according to their aesthetic qualities, yet their real impact occurs not in space alone but in people's interactions with them over time.

It is fairly obvious when designs fail either materially or technically. There have been a number of spectacular collapses of major structures in this country, the most famous of which may be the self-destruction of the Tacoma Narrows Bridge in 1940, filmed by an amateur on the scene.[3] In addition, a number of recently designed buildings have collapsed, seemingly with little external cause, as happened to the roof of the Helmut Jahn–designed Kemper Arena in Kansas City in 1979, just six years after the building was completed.[4] Few would argue that in these cases something fairly significant was overlooked in the design process.

More subtle than the mechanical and technical fitness of a design, but in many cases just as important, are perceptual and experiential considerations; social, institutional, and cultural appropriateness; and environmental responsiveness. In this book I present interviews with some of the most innovative practitioners in design today, each of whose work addresses these more intangible qualities of design success. I order these interviews so that they begin with the smallest and most familiar scale, the design of objects, and end with the largest and most abstract scale, the re-viewing of design itself.

Chapter 1 features a discussion with Michael McCoy, who was cochair of the Design Department at Cranbrook Academy of Art for over two decades. He developed, along with his students, an approach termed *interpretive design,* through which designers use metaphors to infuse meaning into their work. One of the most prominent legacies of the modern movement in design has been the belief in a "universal" grammar of form. However well intentioned, this concept has led to a profusion of anonymous "black box" designs that offer no insight into their purpose or to the process by which they should be used. The aim of interpretive design is to counteract these alienating tendencies of modern design. The significance of this approach is that it goes beyond simple formalism to consider the nature of the interaction between people and designs.

Chapter 2 presents conversations with Daniel Weil and Francis Duffy, each of whom has addressed the need to broaden the scope of design and to articulate a new, more inclusive concept of design professionalism. In recent years design has increasingly fragmented into separate, more inwardly focused and limited disciplines. All of those interviewed for this book have transcended such boundaries, but Weil and Duffy in particular have made the broadening of design knowledge a central part of their work.

Weil is Professor and Course Director of Industrial Design at London's Royal College of Art and a partner in the firm Pentagram Design Ltd. He incorporates knowledge from architecture, art, design, and industry into his objects as part of his exploration of new territories of design. On a larger scale, Duffy, Chairman of London-based DEGW International Ltd. and from 1993 to 1995 President of Royal Institute of British Architects, believes that architects should not just produce new buildings but rather should address what he terms the "choreography of change" within the building stock as a whole. Of particular significance is Weil's and Duffy's recognition that designers should be concerned not just with form fixed in space but with the use of their work over time. Consideration of time poses a whole range of new challenges to designers.

In chapter 3 Belgian architect and town planner Lucien Kroll discusses his work, in which user involvement is central. Often, designers and architects presume what people will like and what will support users' activities without ever checking their assumptions against reality. One reason why many designs fail the test of use is that the designers' suppositions are often wrong. To counteract this, a great deal of discussion in recent years has centered on the importance of user involvement in the design process; yet there are still very few examples of buildings that have been designed using truly collaborative processes.

Kroll has made user involvement his overriding design philosophy. He develops design processes to ensure meaningful collaborations both in new construction and in renovations of failed European housing projects built in the 1960s. Though Kroll focuses on the built environment, his philosophy of user participation is important to all scales and types of designing.

Chapter 4 features conversations with Clino Trini Castelli and Edwin Schlossberg, who, in rather different ways, explicitly address the role of perception in design. Castelli is a Milan-based designer and color consultant who has developed an approach, termed *design primario,* that focuses more on the "soft" qualities of space—light, sound, color, scent, and microclimate—than on form. Schlossberg is President of Edwin Schlossberg Inc. (ESI), a New York–based firm that addresses the role of perception in their design of learning environments such as children's museums, zoos, and interface software. The aim of ESI's work is to create a "conversation" between design and those who interact with it. The significance of Castelli's and Schlossberg's approaches is that with them designs are no longer considered to be formal artifacts but instead are viewed as multifaceted tools of perception.

In Chapter 5 conversations with Kiyoshi Sakashita, Donald Norman, and John Seely Brown are presented; each discusses the approach he has developed to make design more responsive to the context in which it will be used. Sakashita, Executive Director and Head of the Corporate Design Center for Sharp Electronics, coined the term *humanware design* to describe his company's design philosophy, which aims to accommodate the cultural and psychological differences of peoples in various parts of the world. Donald Norman, Vice President for Advanced Technology at Apple Computer and Professor Emeritus of Cognitive Science at the University of California, San Diego, developed the concept of *cognitive engineering,* which uses insights into people's behavior from cognitive science as the basis for design. John Seely Brown, Vice President and Chief Scientist for Xerox Corporation and Director of Xerox's innovative Palo Alto Research Center (PARC), conducts "grounded research" with his team at PARC into the ways in which people understand and interact with the world. This work serves as the basis for the design of "transparent," or easy-to-understand-and-use, high-technology products.

Though an explicit understanding of the "social web" in which design is situated is critical when designing "new technical objects," such as computers, answerphones, fax machines, and the like, the achievement of a "fit" with the social, institutional, and cultural context is also an important element of every successful design. The work of Sakashita, Norman, and Brown offers insights into how context can become a focus of designing instead of afterthought.

Chapter 6 presents conversations with three people who have developed strategic thinking methods: John Thackara, Larry Keeley, and Peter Schwartz. Outside of museums, design books, and magazines, objects are not judged solely by their aesthetic qualities. Instead, they are assessed in terms of the roles they play in larger frameworks of use and meaning. It is necessary, therefore, to think about design in the broadest possible way, and to allow these considerations to influence design development.

John Thackara, who, as mentioned earlier, is Director of the Netherlands Design Institute, has addressed this need for broadly based design thinking directly. He coined the term "Cultural Engineering" to describe the process he uses to bring together teams of designers, clients, and specialists to work on knowledge-based design tasks. Larry Keeley is President of Doblin Group, a Chicago-based firm that has developed an approach termed *strategic design planning*. Using this approach, the firm evaluates the many different factors that influence the production, sale, and use of products and services, and it suggests strategic applications of design effort to help transform their clients' industries in fundamental ways. Outside of the design professions per se, the Scenario Planning approach has been developed by Peter Schwartz, President of the Global Business Network, a consulting firm based in Emeryville, California. This approach permits alternative visions of the future to be envisioned and acted upon. Design has been described as "the performing of a very complicated act of faith,"[5] and so the significance of these strategic thinking methods is clear: by taking into account the broader framework in which design takes place, they enable designers to make better informed decisions.

Chapter 7 features a discussion with John Chris Jones, an industrial designer, educator, writer, and theorist, who re-views some of the underlying assumptions common to design, noting their implications for design decision making. Though designing emerged initially to make objects more responsive to users, it may have evolved to the point where its institutional procedures actually lead to unresponsive design. This transition is especially acute as more design tasks become information based, while traditional design education and processes still primarily address formal concerns. Jones believes that the whole of design activity should be reoriented away from objects and even systems "to the scale of life itself."[6]

As is evident, this book does not focus on any one design discipline, or on any single scale of designing. The ideas raised by those interviewed have value for all design tasks. Taken together, they represent a dramatic shift in the way design is conceived and practiced. As Donald Norman has correctly pointed out, "*Design never ends*. Even the most successful design will have to keep evolving continually in response to new practices."[7] This recognition of the dynamic nature of design in use, which underpins the work of all those featured in this book, will be the distinguishing characteristic of design in the next millennium.

New Thinking in Design

1 | Infusing Meaning

The Modern Movement in architecture and design has been under attack for several decades now, with critics focusing on the rigid and alienating nature of much of the work of that era. One of the first such reactions came from Robert Venturi, who along with his wife, Denise Scott Brown, developed the concept of *postmodernism* in architecture. The key idea underlying their writings and work is that by rejecting the use of all historical references, modern architecture failed to communicate to users. Venturi and Scott Brown reintroduced the explicit use of symbolism, drawn both from architectural history and popular culture, into their work in an attempt to give their designs meaning.

Within product design similar impulses have manifested themselves, though they have been realized somewhat differently. At the scale of objects, it is in some ways even more important that the symbolism used be clear so that people know both what products are and how to use them. This approach to infusing meaning into the design of objects was pioneered by Michael McCoy, who discusses his ideas and work in this chapter.

Michael McCoy: Interpretive Design

Michael McCoy has established himself as a leading designer of products, furniture, and interiors and as an innovator in design thinking and education. He is a partner in two firms: Fahnstrom/McCoy, with Dale Fahnstrom, and McCoy & McCoy, with his wife, Katherine. Among McCoy's clients have been Knoll International, N.V. Philips, Formica Corporation, NEC, and Steelcase. He has received numerous awards for his work, including the European Ergodesign Award (for the Philips Electronic Office System), the Industrial Designers Society of America Gold Medal, and a Japan Design Foundation Award. McCoy's work has also been widely exhibited and published, most notably in the book *Cranbrook Design: The New Discourse.*

Despite the success of his practice, McCoy is perhaps best known for his work during the twenty-four years in which he cochaired, with his wife, Katherine, the Design Department at the Cranbrook Academy of Art. In 1995 they retired from Cranbrook to work independently, though they will also teach one semester per year at the Institute of Design at the Illinois Institute of Technology, Chicago.

The McCoys were instrumental in developing an approach to design termed *product semantics* or *interpretive design.* Though product semantics was much discussed in the 1980s and is often used to describe the work of Cranbrook's students, Michael McCoy shies away from that term now. In our interview, which took place before McCoy left Cranbrook, he explained:

Portrait of Michael McCoy.
(Courtesy Michael McCoy)

> Product semantics is seen by some people as a style that probably would involve maybe wave forms or very obvious similes and analogies formally. The term *product semantics* is actually something that I believe Reinhart Butter cooked up, and we all kind of embraced it as a convenient label. But if you really look at it, it's not a narrow term; it's very broad. It is not at all concerned with a particular or specific product language. It simply says we should all, as designers, be concerned with the meaning of the form that we employ in technology. And that's still true—I think everyone would still agree that that's important.

When asked how he now describes his work, McCoy said:

> Well, I typically use the term *interpretive design,* which to me has a little broader definition: it allows one to look at how people interpret the meaning of things. This is obviously also a concern of product semantics, but would also involve design that specifically tries to engage the users' interpretive powers in some way, more of a negotiation for meaning. If you look through the history of design and architecture that has been influenced by linguistic philosophy—structuralism and poststructuralism—one of the criticisms is

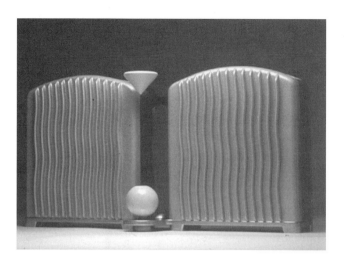

(above left)
Van Hong Tsai, *Toaster*.
(Courtesy Michael McCoy)

(above right)
Paul Montgomery,
Microwave Lunchpail.
(Courtesy Michael McCoy)

that too often it results in "one-liners"—you know, the sort of very obvious analogy or simile. We're much more interested at Cranbrook in work that acknowledges that there is meaning in product form but that doesn't have to be a one-liner. It can be something that unveils itself over time; meaning is partly due to a negotiation between the viewer and the object.

Interpretive Design Philosophy

To better understand interpretive design, I asked McCoy what is being interpreted—technology or the role of a product in people's lives.

> It really depends on the particular object, and it depends on the designer. I think probably one of the key issues we look at is the role of the object in someone's life. The technology then in a sense is a support for that; it's an element of the role of the object in someone's life. For example, if you were designing a home computer you might take a different approach to the technology than if you were designing an office computer because the ritual of use, the kind of routines you go through, and the context that the product is seen in and used in is quite different; the work pattern is different. So an interpretive approach would take into account the context and the kind of ritual or routine of use.

McCoy first became interested in the use of design as an interpretive tool in the late 1970s.

> I started thinking about this whole thing in the seventies when I was on product-design juries, like for *ID* magazine and that kind of thing, and there would just be row after row after row of very nice but basically almost anonymous or identical beige or black boxes, usually beige or grayish—printers and computers and home electronic devices. That really started me thinking about ways of interpreting the individual nature of the object.

Interpretive design has evolved through a number of phases, including consideration of semiotics, poststructuralism, and phenomenology. Asked to expand on how ideas from these fields influence his design thinking, McCoy noted:

Well, actually it's a fairly impure blend; from a scholar of philosophy's viewpoint it would be very imprecise and impure. But basically the early work was very semiotic, very structuralist in nature. A reference point might be some of the earlier work, which was much more specifically analogous and which would be, I would say, structuralist or semiotic work. Then there's a middle range of work, which was still probably not phenomenological—it's still about the symbolism of the piece—but is much more open to interpretation. In other words, it allows a lot more possibilities for interpretation, a lot more paths into the work. I would call that more poststructuralist in nature. And then there is the work that's much more involved with, say, physicality or the body—weight and balance and texture and physical manipulation. That work I would call more phenomenologically based, but it probably also contains elements of poststructuralism.

So you could say the *Phonebook* piece by Lisa Krohn is fairly semiotic in nature; it's an example of the early-to-mid-eighties work. The *Microwave Lunchpail* piece by Paul Montgomery I would say is more poststructuralist in nature. It's a little critical, a little ambiguous—you know, "Is he serious about this or not?" It allows for a lot of interpretations, some of them negative, some of them positive. And then there's something like the round *Pool Computer* by William Wurz composed of pieces you can manipulate. You can approach it from many directions, and I would call that more phenomenological. We had the *Pool Computer* in a show that traveled, and I would hang

Lisa Krohn, *Phonebook.*

(Courtesy Michael McCoy)

out in the museum where the show was being presented, and people really responded to that one. I consider that a real compliment to the project because if it's compelling to people, then I think it's doing its job.

Another phrase McCoy has applied to describe the way in which interpretive design works is *conceal and reveal*. He explained that

> *conceal and reveal* is a poststructuralist term. Semioticians always say that you embed meaning—into a product, for example—and then that meaning is there to be mined and recovered and reconstructed by the audience. So you're placing certain things into the piece, some of which may be immediately apparent, some of which may require living with it for a while and using it. So it really gets back to that idea of a negotiation for meaning between the user and the piece, where things are revealed over time. And actually, in this way you can possibly reveal something about the nature of technology through the design of the piece. This is in contrast to a purely semiotic approach, where a piece's meaning is all there and you get it in about thirty seconds.
>
> In parallel with that, I found it is more difficult to explain some of the later work than, say, the *Phonebook* project. I've noticed this in lectures. If I flash a slide of the *Phonebook* on the screen, or a couple of slides, it's quickly understood. But some of the more (in some ways) sophisticated pieces don't photograph very well, or what it is about them that's interesting is not apparent in the photograph. So when I present them, it takes a lot more discussion. It's more work to communicate what the piece is because it's not intended to communicate immediately.
>
> I think this is a problem in architecture, too. While a lot of the real obvious postmodern work was easy to photograph and communicate in a magazine, a lot of the work that's the most satisfying physically—for example, a building that's not particularly flashy but creates an amazing physical experience of light and sound, smell, and a kind of kinesthetic experience when you're walking through it—you'd never get that from magazine photographs. So it's a limitation of the way we talk about architecture and design professionally—slide shows, magazines, and that sort of thing. It doesn't favor work that is more complex in a sensual way.

Summing up the evolution of his thinking on the subject to date, McCoy said:

> The reason I like the term *interpretive design* is that it also admits the other senses. Semiotics tends to focus on language and symbol, in essence the visual and the linguistic, to the exclusion of all those other things that we know really constitute existence and experience. So I kind of object to a purely linguistic, purely symbolic approach. It's clearly part of it, but it's not the totality of the experience.
>
> When you approach an object, there are a number of these levels of questions. At the simplest level, you ask, "What is it? Just what is this thing?" And

that was the origin of my desire to get away from the "black box," where all products look the same, and to try and get them to identify what they are more effectively. Then at the next level, you ask, "How do I use it? Can a product walk you through its use?" The *Phonebook* is pretty successful there because I think it signals itself as a kind of electronic informational device that's about your personal phone book or your agenda or messages. And then it also then walks you through the use of the product.

Design Education

Many of the artifacts most associated with the evolution of product semantics and interpretive design, such as Lisa Krohn's *Phonebook,* were produced by students in the Design Department at Cranbrook. I asked McCoy how he and his wife, Katherine, were influenced by Cranbrook's distinguished design tradition.

> Kathy and I really feel it's made all the difference for us, once we really started reading and understanding the history and the earlier approaches of Eliel Saarinen, then Eero Saarinen and Charles Eames, Florence Knoll, Harry Bertoia—all these people who were at Cranbrook. They were real believers in design, very passionate believers in design and the role of design and (to use a current term) cultural production. So I think definitely we feel very much influenced by that as well as by an interesting kind of approach to technology that we take here. We're not a technological school in any sense, but we work on high-technology projects, and we use high-technology materials. We just see technology as our clay, as our medium to work with rather than as the determinant of the whole environment.

Describing their teaching philosophy, he said:

> What Kathy and I are primarily trying to do is just set up and maintain a kind of supportive studio platform or environment. People are not necessarily coming here with all of the tools, but the tools are sort of around the studios. Some we teach and some the student culture passes on to itself year after year. If you can get a good student culture going, the new ones coming in can pick up on it from the year before. And they sort of add their twist to it or their extension to it, and they pass it on to the next year.

Asked who sets the agenda for the work in the Cranbrook studios, McCoy explained:

> I think there's a real interaction. I think the students are setting the agenda as often as I am, which is great for me because it keeps me moving. These are graduate students, and a lot of them, most of them, have worked professionally, and they've done some reading and thinking before they've come. So when they get here, they're contributing pretty significantly to the intellec-

tual life of the studio. For me, it's a matter of presenting new ideas to the studio, new readings or new projects while also staying open to and flexible about new ideas.

One of the central aims at Cranbrook has been to encourage students to develop an individual design style. Asked how this can be reconciled with the aim of interpretive design—helping people understand what objects are for and how to use them—McCoy said:

> The idea behind the development of the individual voice is to "humanize" (to take a term that's not all that wonderful). If humanizing technology is a goal, one way to do it is to have evidence of the human hand and the human mind in the form of the products, the design of the software, that kind of thing. That's the aspect of the individual voice that should find its way into technological products. But you don't rely on that entirely. You also use the traditional tools of ergonomics, human factors, those more traditional methodologies that make sure you account for everyone's use patterns, everyone's limitations.

On occasion, Cranbrook student work is criticized for being too fanciful and impractical. It is important, however, to realize that it is, in fact, student work exploring some areas explicitly to the exclusion of others. McCoy agreed:

> Definitely the work is in some cases fairly polemical and not balanced. If you can take these things as experiments and not hard-and-fast solutions, almost like evidence of questions one asks oneself along the way and while working through these problems, then they make more sense. We don't necessarily go for balance in the sense of price, marketing concerns, demographics, design for assembly, those kinds of things. And the reason we don't is that in many cases the students are well aware of and practiced in those sorts of things. But also we want to achieve a kind of intensity in the work, to make a point, really. You may have to sacrifice some other things to do that, always recognizing that the end products have to have a certain balance to them. Actually though, most of the projects are technically quite possible; usually with the prototypes we're just simulating. There's "looks like" and "works like," and we usually separate those two.

A potential limitation of formally based design training is found in its application to newly emerging intangible design tasks such as making computer software. Commenting on this, McCoy said:

> There is a constant discussion here about that. We probably lean toward the object as a polemical device just because it is so, somehow, compelling to people. You can present a written manifesto that says the same thing as, say, that round *Pool Computer,* or you can do the object. It seems from our experience that somehow the object ultimately communicates more. I think in

some cases it's important to emphasize the "objectness" to counteract the kind of insidious nature of technology and microelectronics.

But there are cases, especially if you're talking about cultural or situational things, where a performance might work better, or a video, or a text of some sort. A lot of people here are doing multimedia videos on the computer, and that's opening up some new possibilities—for social commentary, for example. Some pretty good pieces were done about the Iraq war. They were primarily video-sampling and computer-graphic pieces.

If you combine programs like MacroMind Director and some of those multimedia mixing programs and then you connect some MIDI devices, music-generation devices, or sound-manipulation devices—which I'm not particularly good at—you can get remarkable results. We have some students who are incredible; they're virtually wired directly into the machine. The material that's coming out of that is pretty amazing. Some of the students who have graduated are doing music videos. They do them with a combination of the Macintosh and video. So that's a whole new thing—the addition and integration of time into design. In addition, cinematic issues are emerging that are also important in software design. Another big issue here now is interface design. We've worked with Apple and with Nynex and with some other companies on that.

Reflecting on the evolution of his pedagogical approach, McCoy noted:

I would say we were fairly dogmatic to begin with because it was to us a new process. As you do it, you learn gradually that though there are possibilities, there are also limitations. So we've been drifting toward things that have a certain mystery to them—you can't quite get to the edge of it, to define it—which, if you really think about it, is true of those works of art that most all of us consider to be the most potent.

Design Practice

In describing the interrelationship between his teaching and his professional work, McCoy said:

The practice is fairly distinct, but I'll bring projects into the studio if they're not highly confidential. Obviously, the students' ideas affect me and my partner Dale Fahnstrom in Chicago. Since we're working on on-line, direct-commission projects, primarily high-technology products and office furniture, obviously there's a filtration process that goes on. Our work is probably a lot more boring than the student work; but definitely there's an effect there.

Asked how changes such as the advent of flexible manufacturing systems have affected his work, McCoy said:

(above left)
**Fahnstrom/McCoy,
Videophone for Philips.**

(Courtesy Michael McCoy)

(above right)
**Fahnstrom/McCoy,
Bulldog Chair for Knoll.**

(Courtesy Michael McCoy)

The systems we use to control production—the ways we design and engineer, produce and control inventory, and distribute products; also the closer feedback loop between consumers and users and manufacturers—I think these systems lead inevitably towards more customized products. *Customization* is the big word in product design. John Sculley, formerly of Apple Computer, used it as his buzzword in his move towards individualized electronic products, and there's some validity to it, I think.

I'll give you a practical example. We were doing a project for Philips, a video telephone. We decided that although the technical heart of the videophone is the same whether it's in an office or home, if you look at the different contexts and conditions for use, the product should be designed quite differently for those different situations. So we basically did a very simple picture frame with a slot around it, and into this you can plug different elements, some essentially symbolic elements, others functional. So you could really change the videophone quite radically for different contexts. This I saw as a way of customizing a product, a way to take advantage of more flexible manufacturing, order-entry, and inventory-control approaches.

How does McCoy respond when he sees his ideas, or his student's ideas, filtering down into more mainstream consumer products such as AT&T answerphones?

Some of those things look pretty good. I mean, objects have to have form, and objects of a particular year or era have a characteristic look to them, like cathedral radios, or a quality, like streamlining or minimalism. So knowing that's going to happen anyway, it's okay, I guess. If, for example, you were doing a bow shape or a swelling form to indicate something emerging, like a place where you would put a disk into a computer or where sound would be emitted from a speaker, okay. But if that shape was applied to a place where no such thing was happening, then that would be a miscue, I think, a misuse of the language.

Applications and Limitations of Interpretive Design

McCoy's own professional work, and the work of his students, involves three main areas: product design (particularly electronics), furniture, and interiors. Asked whether interpretive design is of particular importance to these areas or whether it has significance for all design tasks, he noted:

> If you take *interpretive design* in the broadest sense of the term, I think it's probably equally important in all realms. I could start an interiors project tomorrow and use a lot of the same attitudes and methodologies that I've been using in a small electronics product. It's actually a methodology, a way of seeing what is important. In the case of an interior, for example, one would address how a public space symbolizes or talks about the cultural condition that supported its making—or just how public space indicates its possibilities for use. Similar interpretive methodologies, or ways of seeing, could be developed for other design realms.

A potential problem with design approaches based on symbolism is that users may not understand symbols as intended. This happened with a prototype for a microwave oven that Philips produced. The product was to sit on the dining-room table and was intended to evoke the image of a Crock-Pot or fondue chafing dish. Unfortunately, the design reminded most viewers of a small nuclear power plant—this at a time when, in the wake of the Chernobyl disaster, Europeans were greatly concerned about the dangers of nuclear power.[1] The prototype was not mass produced. When asked about the potential for designers to invite misinterpretations through use of symbolism, McCoy replied:

> I think if you really take so-called *product semantics* or *interpretive design* the right way, you understand the meaning of the symbols you're using and the meaning of the form. If you understand that form and you do the *Nuclear Power Plant Microwave,* either you know what it means and you're doing it as a critique of microwaves or—if you do it and you're unaware of that implication—you're just not doing a very good job. You could, however, legitimately do a project like that as a cautionary piece.

Design Richness

Asked if there was anything in particular that motivated him to adopt the approach he has taken, McCoy replied:

> If I refer back to the point when I got particularly interested in this approach, it wasn't bad design that motivated me. It was actually a context of highly competent—in conventional terms, fairly "good"—designs such as well-designed boxes and efficiently packaged technology. This work led me to think that, as a profession, we've gotten to a certain point of competency,

which is good. It's actually been a struggle just to get to this point. Now, where do we go from here? Once you achieve the present level, you're free to look around and explore. So my approach is really not so much a critique of where design is or was as it is an examination of the possibilities for growth.

When asked how he approaches his own work, McCoy said:

That depends very much on what the project is. The approach to a piece of emergency equipment is quite different from that toward a glass vase, which you would do as a sort of precious object to be viewed culturally and socially. But I think we try to make products as rich as possible, to be really concerned with how they fit into people's lives at work, at home, and in the public sphere. A lot of products as they're designed are indifferent to that, and if they successfully relate to their public or private environments, they do so almost accidentally. So we try to concern ourselves more specifically with that.

To conclude, I asked McCoy for his definition of good design. He responded:

My idea of a good design is one that is appropriate to its use and its context.

And a good interpretive design?

I would use the same definition, but I would be much more rigorous, especially in terms of use and context. In other words, a good interpretive design really addresses the psychology of use, the cultural context, the way an object makes you feel when you interact with it, or the way an object affects your interaction with someone else.

2 | Increasing Scope

It is said that if the only tool you have is a hammer, then everything you see looks like a nail. In a similar way, designers tend to interpret clients' needs in terms of their own disciplinary focuses. If you are a client with a vaguely defined need for design services, a graphic designer might say that you need a new corporate identity, an architect that you need a new building, an industrial designer that your products need to be restyled. None of these solutions, however, would *directly* address the clients' needs. Instead each of these suggestions is simply a matter of the designer interpreting whatever he or she is presented in terms of his or her own disciplinary orientation.

To combat the increasing fragmentation of the design disciplines, a *metadesign* approach is needed, one that addresses the broader context in which design takes place. Two people who have focused on increasing the scope of design in their work are Daniel Weil and Francis Duffy. In this chapter, conversations with Weil and Duffy will be presented in which they each discuss their work and philosophy of design. Though they have very different points of view, they share a belief in the need for a new, more inclusive, knowledge-based form of design professionalism.

Daniel Weil: New Design Territories

Daniel Weil is a designer and educator born in Argentina and now based in Britain. Like Michael McCoy, he is concerned with overcoming the modernist legacy of anonymous, "universal" design. But whereas McCoy has focused primarily on using design as an interpretive tool, Weil explicitly addresses the relationship of art and industry as mediated through design. In the course of his work, Weil has identified and explored a number of new territories for design activity.

After completing undergraduate studies in architecture at the University of Buenos Aires, Weil moved to London in 1978 to study industrial design at the Royal College of Art. He later became a unit master at the Architectural Association School of Architecture in London and is presently Professor and Course Director of Industrial Design at the Royal College of Art.

In parallel with his studies and teaching, Weil has been active as a designer. Upon graduation from the Royal College of Art, he formed his own design firm, Parenthesis Ltd. He later went into partnership with his former classmate, one-time Memphis group participant Gerard Taylor. Weil is presently a partner in the London office of Pentagram Design Ltd.

Portrait of Daniel Weil.
(Photograph by Martin Dunkerton, courtesy Pentagram Ltd.)

Objects produced by Weil appeared in the 1982 Memphis exhibition in Milan and are in the permanent collections of, among others, the Museum of Modern Art, New York; the Victoria and Albert Museum, London; the Philadelphia Museum of Art; and the Museum of Modern Art, Kyoto.

Architecture, Art, Design, and Industry

Like many Italian designers, Weil studied architecture, then shifted his attention to design tasks on a smaller scale. Explaining this transition, he said:

> I did six years of architectural studies in Argentina, including work in an industrial internship. Before qualifying I worked for a year as a designer in a cutlery factory. Because of this experience, I realized that architecture was, at that point, an experiment in applying formulas. Everything had been done, and the only thing you had to do was to apply the formula given to you. I felt very uncomfortable with that, and I didn't enjoy the idea of being an architect as much as I thought I would like being a designer. That's how it all started, really.
>
> During my internship, I designed some cutlery and a lot of packaging for cutlery. This experience led me to apply to the industrial-design course at the

Royal College of Art, not really understanding at all that, having a full architectural degree, I was a bit overqualified. But I hoped to learn everything there was to be learned about industrial design. The benign system at the college allowed me to develop quite independently. In the three years there, you can really spend a lot of time maturing and developing ideas. I found the environment a very good catalyst. I was also lucky that my three years coincided with a lot of changes in design: postmodernism, Alchimia, Memphis, the Linz exhibition—a lot of quite important landmarks there. This led to the realization that design is not something cast in concrete, that it is there to be repoured in fresh concrete every time. I was lucky to be part of the generation that was making these discoveries. So during the college experience, I worked at what I then considered to be Italian design, doing things that had more presence and personality. They were not just an expression of tooling and mechanical things.

I felt, however, that my last year at the Royal College was really quite limiting. There was an intense feeling that there must be more to design than I was learning. So I set myself the task of learning how to draw—or, at least, improving the way I drew—in a sense, finding a way of representing things differently. Luckily, through life drawing classes I met people in the painting school. A friend introduced me to an essay by Octavio Paz, "The Castle of Purity," about Marcel Duchamp. That really was an amazing sort of eye-opener because it brought together the things I had seen a few years before in the Picasso exhibition in Paris. The Paz essay was about a totally new experience of art, something that was not so visible—about things that were far more invisible. And I worked very hard to try and make a connection to that.

I found that, with a few exceptions, art and design do not cross over very happily. I was in this art-school environment, surrounded by people who were talking about art all the time. And I found that more engaging, actually, than talk about design because the language of design was very poor and uninteresting and fascinated with the microprocessor. When I spoke with fellow designers, we would have these very banal and stupid conversations about people in the future not ever having to queue up, about things that were quite distant in terms of time. We would talk about how the world was going to be "totally transformed." It sounded like social engineering, and it didn't have any intellect to it. It also didn't have any roots, any cultural references. I found the language of communication about design to be a poor one for me. I found more interesting the language of communication about art, which is rich and full of great critics with fresh and stimulating ideas.

That's how I came to create the things I did for my degree show, objects that were very much the development of a process. It was a way of designing where things somehow go through a process of being tested through ideas. I did a series of objects in which I tried to portray the strange and uneasy relationship between art and industry. They were about how industry is experienced as cycles of slow growth, while art moves very comfortably across space and time. Somehow art is not ultimately constrained by the boundaries of centuries, while industry is always linear, sequential. And that was a fundamental thing that stimulated me to make a few objects. I did the radio in a bag and some inflatable radios, and I positioned them in the industrial context though they were born out of art ideas. Meanwhile, the art objects I did were readymades or were formed from industrial components.

So that positioned me, in 1981, in a very different territory in design. The radio in a bag, for example, somehow seemed to communicate something to people. At that moment it made sense because that was the moment of Memphis, and the radio was very different from that. It was not a solid object, it was not in plastic laminate, and it had something to say about the most difficult thing to manipulate at that point—technology. It still is that way, actually, and I haven't succeeded further with it.

The Memphis Exhibition

Following Weil's graduation from the Royal College of Art, he was invited by Ettore Sottsass to prepare a one-man show for the 1982 Memphis collection presentation in Milan. Describing his contribution, Weil said:

> I did a series of objects, the *Tango* radios and *Tempo* clocks, that followed up the inflatable radios. In them the structure was separated from the components; the structure was something you hung things on. This series of objects were both a part of Memphis and a critique of it as well. They were intended to suggest that design remained, that it was about geometric arrangement. The objects were simple, made out of squares and triangles, so you could

(left)
Daniel Weil, *El Ultimo Cafe.*

AM/FM stereo radio from the Tango 2 × 4 series for Parenthesis Ltd., London, 1982. (Photograph by Richard Waite, courtesy Pentagram Ltd.)

(right)
Daniel Weil, *Cambalache.*

AM/FM stereo radio from the Tango 2 × 4 series for Parenthesis Ltd., London, 1982. (Photograph by Richard Waite, courtesy Pentagram Ltd.)

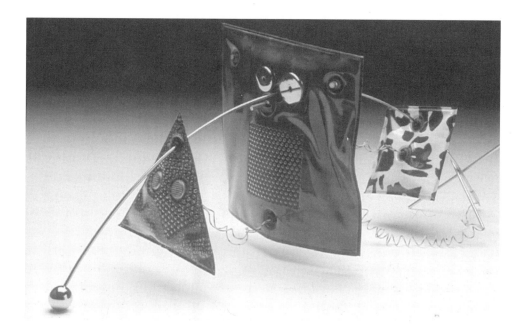

rearrange them and get new ones, very different ones. There were four radios with the same components, but they all had different structures that made them into different objects. They were what Ettore called "dematerialized objects," which I quite liked. In Italian it is a very nice word.

The *Tempo* clocks were very similar. I had some little circuits made that were touch sensitive, so you could bridge the components. I didn't want the clocks to be just art objects. I wanted to produce them consciously as multiples but also to make them technically innovative. I set myself the task of discovering ways to achieve this in every object I produced.

For the radios, I created sandwiches of silk and plastic and made special textures with high-frequency welding. I developed this whole new language of materials, which I felt was quite important. The radios subverted, somehow, the conventional sense of value because silk and plastic do not normally meet. One is a valuable material, the other is not. One of the issues I felt I wanted to address with the radios was the idea of value, because unless that is changed we will have the same dictatorship of convention forever. As long as the way we arrange things in hierarchies does not change, we will be stuck with, say, the idea that heavy things are expensive and light things are cheap; or the idea that things made of plastic are cheap and things made of gold are expensive. So I set out, deliberately, from then on to do a series of objects all around the notion of value.

The *100 Objects* Clocks

Following the Memphis exhibition, Weil undertook a number of commissions. Among his projects at this time was the series *100 Objects,* in which he further explored the relationship of the technical and the aesthetic.

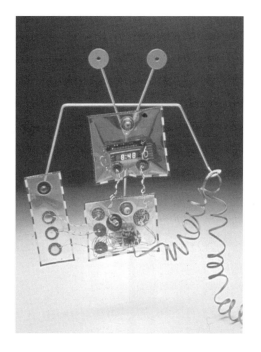

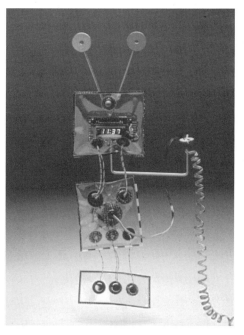

(far left)
Daniel Weil, *Andante*.
Clock from the Tempo *series, with fluorescent display, for Parenthesis Ltd., London, 1982. (Photograph by Richard Waite, courtesy Pentagram Ltd.)*

(left)
Daniel Weil, *Agitato*.
Clock from the Tempo *series, with fluorescent display, for Parenthesis Ltd., London, 1982. (Photograph by Richard Waite, courtesy Pentagram Ltd.)*

I was commissioned to do *100 Objects* by Giuseppe Melzi, a lawyer in Milan. After seeing my exhibition with Memphis, he realized that it would be very difficult for me, because my objects were in another language. He was very interested in it—he's an incredible patron of art—and he just commissioned me to carry on making the multiples, a hundred multiples of whatever I wanted, as a Christmas present for his clients. So I designed that clock, *100 Objects*.

With the money from him, I commissioned an electronics company to manufacture a clock circuit of my own design. I chose components capable of performing a mechanical and an electronic function at the same time. The connector, for example, is also the means of piercing the bag and holding it in a particular form. The plug is the same, as is the jack socket and the buttons, which pierce the bag through standard eyelets. The whole thing is amazing. In this project I found the degrees of freedom that electronic components could give me; basically, the clock is an expression of how far you could, at that point, combine the mechanical and the electronic.

I then pushed onward once more with the next series of a hundred objects. *100 Objects: mirrors of silenced time* was the next clock, so named because with this sort of electronic clock time passes silently, without a tick. I then did another series of the electronic clock with the printed circuit board drawn by hand, discovering a new degree of freedom. This was done to suggest that the engineering aspect of a printed circuit board drawing, with its straight lines, is an arbitrary form. You can actually do the drawing by hand or in any way you want. So I did the printed circuit board like that.

The *Still Life* Series

Weil's next major commission came from the German company Anthologie Quartett, for which he designed a clock. Though commissioned to produce only a single object, Weil expanded the scope of his undertaking into a series of four, which he titled *Still Life*. The remainder he produced independently through his firm Parenthesis Ltd.

> The objects in the *Still Life* series were motivated by my fascination with and real admiration for Cubism, especially the beauty and the immediacy of a lot of Picasso's models and work. I was very interested in trying to use Cubism to incorporate process and time into design. Cubism produces an incredibly clear visual representation; it offers this notion that as a painter you can portray reality through an intellectual game of the two-dimensional and time, actually producing a figurative perspective of what reality looks like. In a way, I associate Cubism with the way designers work. I believe it portrays processes especially well, breaking them up into elevations and plans and sequence. Somehow all the things that surround you are condensed in a still life.
>
> The first of these objects was the clock for Anthologie Quartett, titled *Hinge*. It is quite a central, important object. The idea is that since time is passing in the real clock, it's not a still life. It's an object balanced between an existence as a mechanical readymade and an artistic, human side. And there's a little invention in the face of the clock: the numbers are printed in front of

(left)
Daniel Weil, *Hinge.*

Clock designed for the Still Life series for Anthologie Quartett, Germany, 1984.

(Photograph by Richard Waite, courtesy Pentagram Ltd.)

(right)
Daniel Weil, *Walter.*

A vase from the Still Life series designed for Parenthesis Ltd., London, 1984.

(Photograph by Richard Waite, courtesy Pentagram Ltd.)

Daniel Weil, *Claire*.
A fruit bowl from the Still Life series designed for Parenthesis Ltd., London, 1984.
(Photograph by Richard Waite, courtesy Pentagram Ltd.)

the hands and in a soft medium, which is a nice reference to an artist I don't like too much, Dali. But it was really interesting to discover that I could put the Dali reference in a context that works for me.

Continuing the *Still Life* series, I then did *Walter* and *Claire* on my own. The names *Walter* and *Claire* I had used before in another context; they were my average consumers, characters created for my degree show. Designers used to believe that the consumers they were designing for did not have any taste, that as manipulators, designers were in the business of dictating what consumers should like. Hence the pun for these consumers with no taste was without any taste, or insipid. Just as water and air do not have any taste, so Walter and Claire, my average consumers, were tasteless.

And they came back. *Walter* is the flower vase. It reconstitutes a Cubist still life, a typical café scene with a wine glass by Braque or Picasso or Gris. *Walter* came back as a flower vase because this is a traditional still life. You have flowers, you have seasons. I just brought the notion of the still life into three dimensions. It had to be a real thing, an object that could be functional, have a purpose, and be capable of holding flowers. So the wine glass became the flower vase. And then *Claire* is "air," and it is a fruit bowl that's at a tilted angle, using gravity to actually hold the fruit in an "avalanche barrier" of wire mesh.

To conclude the series, I did a fourth piece, a radio titled *Small Door*. This object was an attempt to prove that somehow there is another element in reality. There is space, and there is no better way of portraying space than with sound. So the radio was there for a purpose and not only because I knew that I could make radios work. (Though that has been always an important thing to me; I think in everything I did I wanted to make it work, even if it was very, very simple.)

Small Door is a simple object, just the opposite of *Claire*. It tries to suggest that gravity does not matter in the case of a radio. The only important aspect of gravity was the physical consequence of it, so I put a piece of fabric over the speaker. I wanted it like a veil over the speaker, one that would move with the speaker, ideally—though obviously the speaker is not powerful enough. I was interested in transforming the fabric into some sort of sculpted material. Since it just stays there, static, you might as well have it carved. The rest of the radio was to be like a landscape. On top I wanted a landscape with knobs. I worked with a readymade circuit, made the simplest of protective cages around the circuit, and hung the battery from the legs. Originally I had the idea of doing a full-size door radio. But as my intention has always been to produce objects that are small-scale and easily transportable, the final object had to be small. That's why it's called *Small Door.*

You can see that each one of the pieces in the *Still Life* series has its own little world because they had to be objects in their own right. They were not designed as a collection or as a set whose styles are rigidly connected. They were intended to be metaphorically connected, and tenuously visually connected. For example, the flowers in *Walter* are supposed to be on the same level as the speaker of *Small Door,* which has fabric covered with flowers.

As reflected in these comments, one key aspect of Weil's work is that, though he begins with scores of drawings, he physically produces the prototypes—and in some cases whole sets of objects—himself.

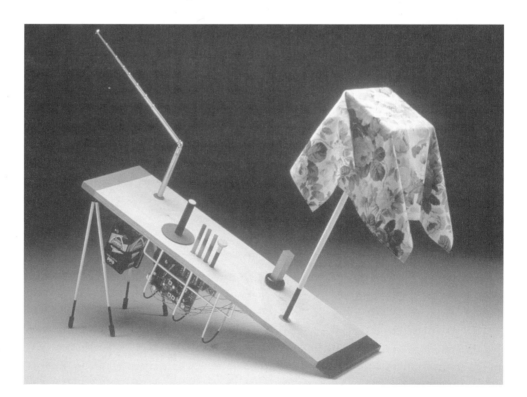

Daniel Weil, *Small Door.*

Three-band radio from the Still Life series, designed for Parenthesis Ltd., London, 1984. (Photograph by Richard Waite, courtesy Pentagram Ltd.)

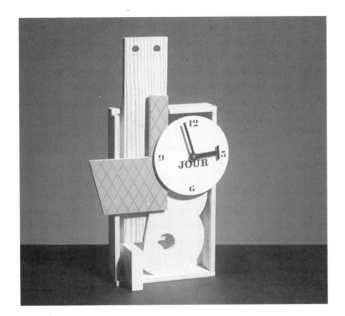

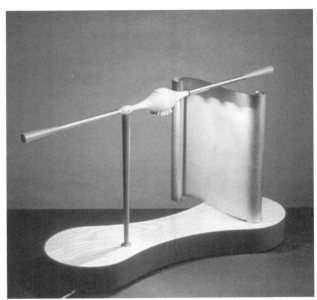

In the case of *Hinge,* I said, "At this point I don't have many tools. If I make it with materials from the Do It Yourself shop around the corner, it will be the best way of dealing with the brief." So that's how I did it and why it is made of plywood, and why there's a thumb bolt and a washer and simple screws—nothing too sophisticated.

I wanted *Hinge* to be a low-complexity object so I could manufacture it, because I made almost everything myself. Some parts were made for me, like the plates for the fruit bowl; they were even laser cut at some point. The rest I made myself, though I did have some assistance. It was very important to be close to the materials, and understanding it was an important part of the experience. Getting my hands dirty was important. It's also part of the learning and development of a designer.

(above left)
Daniel Weil, *Jour.*
Clock for Anthologie Quartett, Germany, 1987.
(Photograph by Richard Waite, courtesy Pentagram Ltd.)

(above)
Daniel Weil, *H'Arp.*
Table lamp for Anthologie Quartett, Germany, 1987.
(Photograph by Richard Waite, courtesy Pentagram Ltd.)

In addition to *Hinge* from the *Still Life* series, Weil undertook a number of other commissions for Anthologie Quartett, collaborating at times with partner Gerard Taylor. These projects include *Jour,* a clock derived from Cubist compositional ideas; *H'Arp,* a table lamp; a series of tables, one each for wine, fruit, and flowers; and *Kind-Size,* a series of furniture for children. Describing these projects, Weil said:

Somehow that work served both as pieces of production and as academic pieces, because I did the things to try to push design further and to conquer small new territories—to put ideas in, because I believe that design is about putting in as opposed to extracting.

Most recently, as a partner in Pentagram Design Ltd., Weil has been working on a range of projects, including concepts for Legoland in Denmark, work for Polaroid, and a CD cover for the British pop group Pet Shop Boys.

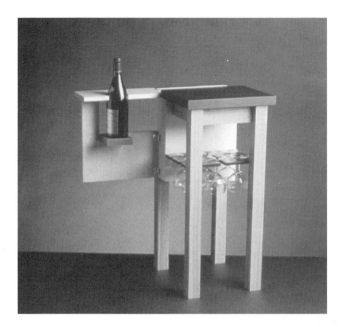

The *Light Box*

The projects that perhaps most clearly reflect Weil's design approach were under-taken while he was an instructor at the Architectural Association. At that time Weil prepared an exhibition of his work, titled *Heavy Box,* to be presented at the AA. To accompany the exhibition, he produced a catalog/object titled *Light Box.* Describ-ing this, Weil said:

> The *Light Box* was a catalog for an exhibition, but I designed it as an object in and of itself. It portrays all those things that I then thought to be relevant to the design process—my design process, not some universal one. The only thing I can do is just offer and show my design process, and if others can identify themselves with it and if they want to use part of it, so be it. I think each process has its own timing, its own way of triggering thought, and in my case things that are important were represented there.
>
> The manipulation of material and the industrial process is represented especially in the hand-drawn printed circuit board. There is the *One Yard of Fabric,* which has the drawings of the *Still Life* series on it. Then there are drawings behind a wooden patterned envelope with holes in it that actually holds the drawings inside. And then there is a sketchbook in the shape of a palette, a wooden palette like a painter's palette. It's a portrayal of "little art," art with a small *a,* where ideas happen. And inside, there is a chessboard with instructions to collect the chess set made out of readymade, hardware pieces.

Addressing the significance of his instructions for a readymade chess set, Weil said:

Think of the chess set made by Josef Hartwig of the Bauhaus, which was designed in such a way that the pieces show how they move on the board. The square at the top is for one move, the cube at the top for another. Then you have a cube with a little piece missing, and that odd shape is for the way the knight moves. In contrast, the chess pieces in the *Light Box* are pieces of hardware that reflect the new layer that we deal with when we're designing now. We cannot bring life into the game of chess without going into figuration. Josef Hartwig sort of abstracted it all with little figures to make it purely Design Meets Chess. But I think that my chess set tries to say Design Meets Chess and Then Meets Life Again. The whole thing is one, so the complexity is larger. Also, the chess pieces themselves show how we as designers have to deal with design, how it's not good enough anymore just to look at a pure, isolated issue as if dealing purely with a service. The idea is that you can't design a chess set only looking at chess; you have to bring life into it. The context is much larger. There's no such thing as a small project anymore. We have to bring reality in.

Beyond Problem Solving

When asked for his views of what good design is, in terms of his own work, Weil responded:

To do design as problem solving is one thing, but to do good design is quite another. I cannot say that what I do is good design, but I hope it is about actually "putting in," for other people to be able to see and understand something else. And that's how I think good design is defined—that other people will use it as a tool to understand further and to go further. Otherwise it's service, really, and I think design is not *just* service, otherwise it wouldn't be defined as a profession. It's true that design is still seeking to gain knowledge, like any other profession we need knowledge. The problem is we are an infant profession and we're not ready to ossify knowledge yet. We're still flexible and changing and being made aware of the changes in technology, changes in lifestyle and the changes in communication and media, and so on.

While I believe that architecture is mother of the arts—it's the origin of design as an experience—I also believe that it has relinquished the position of the encompassing and general discipline. The general practitioners of design are not the architects anymore, because they have other concerns. Architecture is reducing in complexity, it's more about buildings, less about the whole. Somehow I believe that one of the design disciplines has to start to hold the whole; the closest we've come to this has been in two dimensions, for example with logos and corporate identity, strategy, and thinking about communications. It's all about the whole picture.

But there's nothing in three dimensions like that, no understanding of the big context, which is what architecture traditionally did. I believe that that's the role of industrial design. The people who work in three dimensions need to move away from just being a service and understand the bigger picture. So it's all about understanding the context instead of just purely designing a solution according to what has been designed before in a similar area.

What has happened is that designers are accustomed to the one-to-one scale, but when it starts to go large they're a bit lost. So it's quite important to work more conceptually on the bigger pictures. Then they will find it a lot easier to discover more complexity in what they're doing. It's important that we put more complexity and a bit more intellect into the activity of designing, and the activity of encouraging other designers by doing so.

My students, for example, do not present their work by showing an elevation or a sketch or a magic marker rendering and a model, all of which are doing exactly the same job. They're actually working on representation, they're working on how to draw ideas and so when they show the models of the final things they have other things to explain. The experience of designing is rich, it's not just the final object for designers. This is very, very important. In the manufacturing process, and even in the selling today, you have to have a story. Nothing is isolated anymore, everything is about communication. So what the hell, we have to develop that process, the capacity to communicate with each other as designers with a language that is not just the client language. Architecture developed its own language and I believe while we do have jargon for design, we don't have enough. We don't communicate enough how we do it and what we're interested in.

To help us with this I think that design history is superrelevant, in the same way I think art history is superrelevant. I referred earlier to the notion of knowledge. We are trying to accumulate knowledge, and knowledge is not just purely technical data, but it is the sort of subjective way in which we make decisions. What are the things that trigger us to make those decisions and in what way do we make them as cultured people? Maybe Alvar Aalto did something relevant, maybe it was Frank Lloyd Wright. We would be better off to try and hold a bit more of the inferences alive in the same way that artists do. Art does this very comfortably.

Every time design happens as if it was an expression of technical data, it is spiritless. I think designing is about touching people. And the problem with design is that you have to be touched by people; in that sense that it's difficult to learn just purely from a magazine of the moment. You must say how did you get that knowledge? And what influenced you that you thought was so good that you were struck by it? Otherwise it's purely problem solving, and engineers are much better at that for sure.

Francis Duffy: The Choreography of Change

Frank Duffy is a cofounder and Chairman of DEGW International Ltd., a 150-person firm with offices in eight countries. Over the past two decades, DEGW has conducted research and provided design services for a wide range of clients, including the British government, Arthur Andersen, British Airways, IBM, Lloyds Bank, Lloyd's of London, The Prudential, and Steelcase. In addition, Duffy recently completed a two-year term as President of the Royal Institute of British Architects, that country's professional body.

Portrait of Francis Duffy.
(Courtesy DEGW)

Before beginning his professional career, Duffy undertook extensive studies. He received an honors diploma from the Architectural Association School, London, before undertaking graduate studies as a Harkness Fellow at the University of California, Berkeley, and at Princeton University. In his dissertation Duffy investigates the effect of organizational theory on the design of office buildings. This extensive academic background reflects Duffy's belief in the importance of research on building use as a basis for design, a focus that is central to all of DEGW's work.

In describing the scope of the services that DEGW offers, Duffy said:

> Our work is narrow in some ways but very wide in others. We rarely wander away from the design of the workplace, so there's a very strong focus on designing office workplaces, buildings, and interiors. We're focused sharply on one area of work, although within that we go pretty deep. The reason for this is that the firm's history is very much based upon user research. We've always tried, in parallel with design practice, to understand why people want things and what they want and what the trends are. So from the very beginning in 1971, we have managed to maintain an investigation of how the workplace is changing. We've managed to build up a knowledge base on that, and our design is closely influenced by that database. Our design reputation comes directly from research interest, which while not unique is unusual. Other people have done similar work in schools in this country and in hospitals particularly, but we've decided, for one reason or another, to concentrate on offices.
>
> At one end of the spectrum, we design and program furniture. For example, there's the furniture we've designed for the Swedish firm Facit, called *Facit iO,* which deals particularly with service distribution but which has turned out to be quite handsome. We designed that with Knut Holscher, the Danish architect. It's an example of our product-development work. We also prepare graphics and design other information—for example, books and pamphlets that describe our architectural projects and help users understand what they're for. Then we design interiors. A big example is the project we're

DEGW with Knut Holscher, view of the Facit iO System.

The furniture is designed to accommodate individual and collaborative work.

(Photograph by Arne Flink, courtesy Facit Office Furniture, Denmark)

(below)
DEGW with Knut Holscher, view of the Facit iO System.

(Photograph by Arne Flink, courtesy Facit Office Furniture, Denmark)

(below right)
DEGW with Knut Holscher, view of the Facit iO System.

The furniture was designed to accommodate changes in the use of information technology.

(Photograph by Arne Flink, courtesy Facit Office Furniture, Denmark)

just finishing for The Prudential insurance company in London. We've done a lot of work for Lloyd's of London and Lloyds Bank. It's been a very, very important part of our work—large-scale interior design. We also do space planning, which doesn't necessarily connect with physical realization. Space planning depends on a careful collection of information about where furniture goes and how people occupy space. We do programming, as well, a lot of programming work—sometimes for new buildings, sometimes for space standards, sometimes on a global scale. We've been working, for example, on Arthur Andersen's global space guidelines recently.

Then we do architecture. An example of this is the new pathology laboratory for a famous children's hospital in London, the Great Ormond Street Children's Hospital, which is under construction. At any one time, we usually have one or two architectural projects in the office. They're very important to us. And we do urban design. That's usually concerned either with the

regeneration of the inner city or with business parks. That kind of work is being done across Europe, in France and Germany, as well as in the UK. I think that's about everything, except for research. Usually we have a multi-client research project on the go, which allows us to examine a new area of development in the office field. Research work is really the generator of most of the other things. Our strength, our reputation, our ideas come from those research projects.

When asked how the areas which DEGW researches are chosen, Duffy responded:

> Our research direction stems from the interests, the enthusiasms of the people in the firm. We're not a very large firm. We are very much driven by the kind of projects people want to follow up. Most people in DEGW have a notion about what's important to them. They have always tried to get together research projects, and you find that continuity of investigation has influenced our design. It doesn't always work out, but we try to get design projects that illustrate or illuminate or carry forward the work that's been done on the research side. In addition, we are fairly self-conscious about the training programs we run in the firm. We try to make sure that everyone in the firm understands what's going on and sees the connection between the ideas and the physical reality.

(above left)
DEGW, view of the atrium area at Prudential Headquarters Building, Holborn Bars, London.

(Photograph by Nicholas Kane, courtesy DEGW)

(above)
DEGW, view of the mezzanine office area of the Corporation of Lloyds 58 Building, London.

(Photograph by Graham Challifour, courtesy DEGW)

DEGW, view of the general office area at Prudential Headquarters Building, Holborn Bars, London.

(Photograph by Nicholas Kane, courtesy DEGW)

In fact, that goes back to the dual nature of the firm, programming/research and design. It would have been possible, easily possible, to have invented a design firm that didn't have a research component. And it would have been possible, downright normal in fact, to have invented a consultancy research firm that didn't have a design component. But from the very beginning, we decided we wanted both—and both simultaneously, so that one could feed off the other. Feeding one off the other is achieved by individual enthusiasms, by constant internal dialog, and by the training program that

DEGW, view of the board room at Prudential Headquarters Building, Holborn Bars, London.

(Photograph by Nicholas Kane, courtesy DEGW)

DEGW, elevation of the Great Ormond Street Hospital, London.
(Courtesy DEGW)

we use to unite all our offices and to bring people up to date. And there's a fourth factor, which is that we talk a lot to the outside world through our writings. All these ideas are tried out internally before they become public.

One of the first major multiclient research projects initiated by DEGW was the ORBIT study of the impact of information technology on office buildings in England, completed in 1983. Later ORBIT studies included assessments of offices in North America and Japan. Duffy's firm has continued to undertake this kind of study. Commenting on the most recent ones, he said:

> "The Responsible Workplace" was a multiclient study done in 1991/92 that has now been published in book form. Slightly later is a study called "The Intelligent Building in Europe." This is an attempt to describe the features of the intelligent building in the European context. We're plotting two or three other multiclient studies at the moment. One is likely to be on the way in which office buildings are serviced, and how that's going to change as space-use intensification and new patterns of work develop. That's something we'll likely do with the Building Research Establishment, which is a government research facility here with whom we did "The Responsible Workplace."
>
> We also have an ongoing, extremely useful body, a kind of club, called The Workplace Forum, which has about eighteen members, all large corporate clients, often European-wide. Generally, they meet once a quarter, and then

we have a two-day workshop once a year where we present papers to them. The corporate clients' motive is to keep in touch with the field in a non-threatening, well-organized way. Our motive, of course, is to keep in touch with leading-edge thinking among our clients in as formal a way as possible. And there is the desire, the strong desire on the part of our clients, for bench-marking, so that they can formally compare their performances as managers and as space users. They want to know how to improve their particular facilities in relation to those of other leaders in the field. The Workplace Forum is a tremendously important institution for us, and we're going to try and make that grow and develop. It's been around for a few years now.

DEGW, "Rethinking Office Space" diagram.

(Courtesy DEGW)

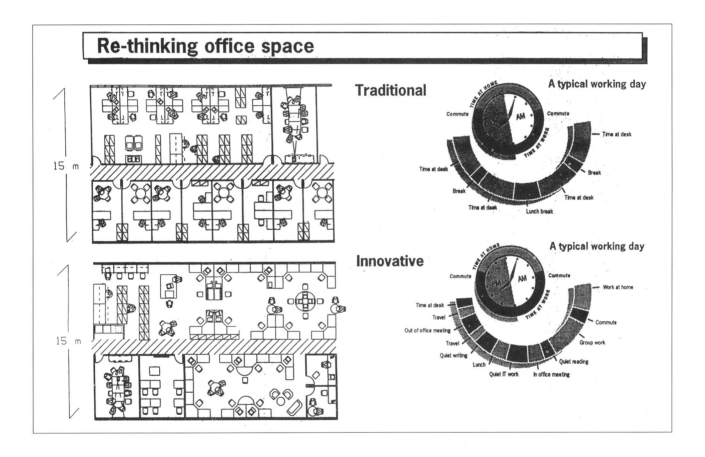

Intelligent Building

Not surprisingly, the extensive research that DEGW conducts on how information technology impacts office design has made the firm a leader in the design of "intelligent buildings" in Britain and the rest of Europe.

Our work in the intelligent building field has two characteristics. First, it's based on extremely user-sensitive research in our tradition. Second, it's based upon the idea that intelligence, real intelligence, lies in the "software" of space management as much as the "hardware" of buildings or electronic

DEGW, page from "Office Facilities Guide."

(Courtesy DEGW)

Meeting areas

LARGE CONFERENCE ROOMS

- Do you really need them?
- Dual use for boardroom, training, and formal conference needs
- Appropriate quality levels
- Practicality and flexibility of planning
- Storage of equipment and furniture
- Variation of equipment requirements
- Proximity to break areas and telephones
- Consider use of public off-site facilities

GENERAL MEETING ROOMS

- Durable and flexible furniture with particular reference to working surfaces
- Consider implications of change of use over time
- Potential office automation and cabling requirements
- Can be used as project rooms
- Minimal and thrifty outfitting
- Ensure optimum sizes to allow for sensible and realistic layouts with adequate chair clearances

INFORMAL MEETING AREAS

- Durable furniture
- Location should not be disruptive
- Opportunity to create more open plan space between enclosures
- Encourage positive interaction when in office
- Support use of open-plan workstations

gadgetry of buildings' fabric. How those things are managed is what matters. That's very much our approach to building intelligence. It's easy for us now to rate the capacity of buildings to respond to change, not least with built-in electronic devices. That connects with space planning, of course, and so it becomes easier and easier to relate buildings to corporate goals, to the real business of the organization. What are organizations on this planet for? What are they doing? Our concept is firstly "software" oriented and only in a secondary sense "hardware" related.

Duffy was one of the first to apply the concept of *software* to the analysis of architecture, having done so in the late 1970s. Expanding on this, he noted:

It's an interesting analogy and an important one, I think, for architects. They need to understand what it means for them and how it affects the services we offer. It's essential to get architects to understand the importance of designing the use of space through time. This concept allows architects to deal with questions of obsolescence; it allows us to deal with the way in which buildings mature; it allows us to deal with managerial issues; it gives us much, much greater scope than we would have otherwise as designers.

The great thing about being our sort of firm, very much user based and client oriented, is that it entails living in the real world with real clients who are getting more and more sophisticated and more demanding. Once you've seen clients stimulated by design ideas, it's impossible not to work better for them. Clients want that. They're happy you understand what they've seen themselves, that what they want is the design of space through time. So we don't find it too difficult to respond in this way. We're responding to demand, real demand.

Architectural Specialization

Though the focus of DEGW's work has from the outset been on user-centered research and design, the firm has actually worked in conjunction with some of Britain's best-known, more visually oriented architects. Commenting on the relationship of his firm's work to that of architects such as Richard Rogers and Norman Foster, Duffy noted:

Our work is complementary. We've worked with both of those architects at the programming/space planning side, at the early stages and at the user stages. They use us to be their interface with clients because we have superior skills in that particular respect. They recognize that, and I think they feel happy working with us because we save them a lot of time. In the history of the firm, such relationships go right back to the beginning, twenty years ago. We're always very happy to work with such architects in a specialized role. I suspect that's unusual for architects; I don't think many architectural practices do that. We do like working with them—it's a tremendous extension of our expertise. We're on extremely good terms with most of the big-name British architects, in fact. It's the less-good architects we have trouble with because they're much more nervous about their position. The good ones who are totally confident about their design skills are relaxed enough to cope with specialization.

So I don't think there's any real conflict. If you get everything aligned and see things correctly, there's no conflict between us and other architects. It's only when you begin to suboptimize and say, "You can only have this" or "This is the only way in which I'm prepared to work" that you become weak. Then you begin to block out opportunities rather than to increase opportunities—which is what design should be about. Design is about imagining future scenarios and making future scenarios possible.

Commenting on the way DEGW goes about providing specialized architectural services, Duffy said:

When you look at the way we're structured as an office here, there are some people who are obviously much happier dealing with details and other people who are very happy with project management, getting things done on site. Some people are good detail space planners, and other people are good conceptual researchers. Not everyone has got all the skills. One of the chief characteristics of DEGW is that we've always tried to respect, within a common framework, the fact that all of us are more or less defective. No one of us has the whole range of ability. Just admitting that is a tremendous step forward.

In relation to the wider question of architectural education, there's a big lesson that's got to be learned. We're all going to be more and more dependent on a knowledge base. Not everyone can enjoy the whole knowledge base. Architectural training will become, especially at the later levels, more and more specialized. Schools will have to cope with one, two, or three facets of architectural knowledge rather than attempt to deal superficially with the whole. A present weakness in architectural education is the habit of focusing on one type of architecture to the exclusion of all others. What should be common to all architects is the ability to imagine a future state and to determine how that future state should be achieved. That is what I mean by *design imagination*. That seems to be the architect's essential quality.

In addressing the current state of architectural education, Duffy noted:

Presently there's a lot wrong with architectural education, of course, but there are structural reasons for some of our problems. It's very, very hard to simulate the client in the studio. There are certain things you can learn with studio teaching, but to learn how to be a real architect is difficult. We're talking about a quite complex set of variables. To add the dimension of time and change makes the teaching task even more complicated. These are relatively new ideas that will take some time to work their way into the architectural vocabulary.

Metadesign

In addition to developing architectural specialization, one of the central features of DEGW's work has been the incorporation into the architectural design process of knowledge from related design disciplines.

To me, both facilities management and interior design are part of the design program, and to that extent part of the architectural program, although obviously formally not always linked. They are part of our great, ongoing architectural tradition. Now there's the big and fascinating question about boundaries, about who belongs and who doesn't belong to the world of architecture. I don't know what the answer is, but it seems to me the opposite of rational to regard such areas of activity as being totally separate from architecture. I'd rather work with them and think about the boundaries afterwards than work within our own boundaries and reject them. They've got a hell of a lot to teach architects, these interior designers and facilities managers. Alliances are what I'm into, not dogfights.

Within these alliances of design disciplines, architects, in Duffy's view, have unique skills, an opportunity, and an obligation to help resolve the interrelationships between information technology, organizational structures, and buildings. Asked about the nature of the relationship between these elements, Duffy said:

I had an interesting conversation about this at lunchtime with someone from the world of information technology (IT), from Digital Equipment Corporation, as well as a management consultant and myself. We were speculating about the changing nature of work and how quickly organizations are going to realize that they can manage the design of the use of space.

We were also trying to think what are the reasons for the inhibitions, the blocks that are very evident at the moment. Neither architects, nor IT people, nor organization theorists are powerful enough to be able to manage change. We were speculating that the inhibitions probably arise because all three things are dealt with separately. You can only do so much with IT as a generator of change, you can only do so much with organizational structure as a generator of change, and you can only do so much with buildings to generate change. If you deal with all three together, if you find a way, a real "meta-role" in which all these things can be somehow coordinated, then probably change would be facilitated, change would be accelerated, and the excesses and waste and redundancy that are characteristic of the office environment would be removed.

That's why using programming and design together is so important: You can make sure the architectural imagination is somehow captured by what information technology can do and that information-technology people also understand what architects and organizational structure can do. How do you get all these things working together? What kind of discourse is necessary to despecialize? I want specialization on one hand and despecialization on another to get everything working together.

Citing one case on which DEGW is presently involved, Duffy said:

We're currently doing some wonderful work for Arthur Andersen in which that whole organization is thinking about space, spatial resources, information technology, and how to manage them in a very interesting and challenging way. So when the organizational imagination catches fire, it's absolutely marvelous. It's tremendous. That's why I think clients are so important, because they actually want things to happen.

The Future of Architecture

In his roles as Chairman of DEGW, with its ongoing research into the changing nature of design, and as President of the Royal Institute of British Architects, Duffy has thought about the future of architecture in some detail. Commenting on the potential impact of some major trends that are emerging, such as time-sharing and virtual offices, Duffy said:

> Well, the implications of those ideas are absolutely tremendous, certainly from a developer's point of view, because they relate to the design of the whole building stock. How much space do we have in the design of cities? How big should Dallas be? What separation should there be between home and work? What boundaries should there be in the city? What kind of office space should there be? These are fantastically important, imagination-searing questions, and we simply must address them at this stage in development of the city.
>
> There could not be a more interesting issue than the changing nature of work. What's happening now is really equivalent in scale to what happened at the end of the nineteenth century with the invention of new forms of technology and new forms of organizational structure, with Taylorism and the typewriter and the telephone. It's as important as that. We are, this decade, going to work out what cities of the twenty-first century will be like. It's within our power to imagine it, and we've got to do it.
>
> What has to be done is twofold: partly to imagine the future and also partly to preserve and honor the past. There's a continuity there. I think one of the many mistakes that architects make is to think we're the custodians of only new buildings. Actually we're not; we're the custodians of the whole stock, *all* buildings, and it is a design matter to work out how they should be managed and used through time. There are lots of ways in which architectural imagination has artificially narrowed its focus in the last few decades.

Though numerous disciplines will be involved in the transformations to come in the next few years, Duffy insists that:

> The power lies with the people who are doing the work, the actual end users. As you've probably seen from my book *The Changing Workplace,* social democracy at work has a tremendous impact upon the shape of northern European office buildings. People are really where the power lies. The rest of us are just serving those emerging requirements. That's why I'm so keen on the methodology of building appraisal: we've got to measure the capacity to buildings to accommodate change; we've got to find a way of drawing the trajectory of organizational change, of measuring what the features of change are, and of finding ways in which those changes can best be accommodated in buildings—determining which buildings accommodate change best. This is an analytic but also forward-looking style of architectural thought.

Expanding on this approach, Duffy said:

> Postoccupancy evaluation is obviously a part of this, but only a part. We also need the projection of organizational structures and user requirements into the future. We need a methodology of constantly understanding, projecting, and feeding back, of relating existing stock and new stock to changing needs. This process is very close to what I understand by architecture. Whether one is a provider, developer, architect, or project manager, one's got to make it clear where we stand on all this. The relationship is a kind of dance rather than a static situation. It's the choreography of accommodating change.

Design Professionalism

Given the changing nature of the built environment, this is a particularly critical moment in which the architectural profession must redesign itself in order to respond to the new challenges that are presenting themselves. As President of the Royal Institute of Architects, Frank Duffy helped frame the terms of this reconceptualization of the profession in Britain. Matters were further complicated there by government proposals to scale back architectural education and to remove the legal protection of the term *architect*. Duffy's inaugural lecture as RIBA president, titled "A Defence of Professionalism," signaled his intention to vigorously oppose these proposed changes. Duffy's campaign to resist these changes was ultimately successful.

> In the U.K. we have protection of title. We don't have, as you do in the United States, protection of function. That's been the situation since the 1930s. So the title, *architect,* is protected but nothing else is. Anyone can put buildings forward for planning permission. We have no monopoly on architectural skills. But the institute has decided to resist deregistration quite vehemently. It's not as simple as saying we want things to be as they were in the past. It's much more complicated than that. We have success-fully created what is in many ways an excellent educational system, which is being threatened, but also we're under tremendous economic pressure, competitive pressure, which is actually resulting in all kinds of absurdities in the ways we deliver buildings.
>
> I argued in my inaugural address that these attacks are part of the collapse of belief in professionalism. Professionalism depends on a body of knowledge about what *ought* to be. This is not just to do with the market; this is not knowledge in the academic sense. This is about the application of deontic knowledge in the context of action. Future-seeking knowledge is what the professional bodies of medicine, law, and architecture are really all about. That kind of knowledge can only be developed within a robust, independent, autonomous, professional framework such as we invented in the Anglo-Saxon world two hundred years ago. It's one of the world's great inventions, and we should fight hard before we let it be damaged or distorted or diminished in any way.

Though he strongly supports the concept of architectural professionalism, Duffy is by no means uncritical of recent trends in architecture.

> Taking the RIBA first, we're still short of intellectuals. We need a lot more high-level intellectual activity in order to get us where we want to be. But let's hope we'll be able to continue to change the RIBA, to make it more lively. Certainly Richard MacCormac, my predecessor as president, did an enormous amount in that respect. There's always a conservative force in such organizations, but times are so desperate that I think it's probably the best moment for achieving change that one could possibly imagine. We've got to do something better than we've done in the past. Otherwise we won't be here.

Another challenge is the public disenchantment with architects and architecture, which has become more vocal in recent years, with Prince Charles being among the most outspoken critics in Britain. Addressing the prince's role in the architectural debate, Duffy noted:

> In terms of the prince and his influence and the people who surround him, I think they are taking an important part in architectural discourse. It's fascinating to see how the prince's new school of architecture is developing, to follow the issues that are being addressed and the kind of tensions that are being dealt with and the forms that are emerging. It's quite a rich mixture, not at all a reduction of architecture to one kind of "right style" as opposed to other "wrong styles," as one might have thought. I shall be delighted to see it develop. I think the prince has done architects a good turn actually by raising architecture on the public's agenda in this country.

When asked if he agreed with those who have criticized the prince's book *A Vision of Britain* for proposing a style and not dealing with some of the structural problems faced by architects today, Duffy said:

> I think he's open to that criticism because I don't think he's always sensitive to the whole breadth of the debate in architectural thought. That's a pity. Nevertheless, prince or not, once you start thinking along these lines, there's a sort of intellectual dynamic that works its way through everything. I think the prince too is caught up in this extremely important and interesting debate. He's very influenced by Chris Alexander of course, and Alexander's a very important, extremely influential, very subversive figure in the architectural firmament, and has been for a long time. When you think in this kind of way, you can't simply stick to one style or one manner of doing things. You become a varied, complicated, metaphysical person. That Alexandrian component of the prince's thought is extremely interesting. I'm very sympathetic to it. How it can be made to coincide with a love of Georgian England is a fascinating question that I think is by no means answered. The debate goes on, the jury's still out.

Maturing, Diachronic Design

One of Prince Charles' primary criticisms has been of the acontextual imposition of modern buildings into Britain's historical town centers. Addressing this, Duffy noted:

> When the history of the twentieth century is written, I really do wonder what it will say about why the disasters of the sixties and seventies happened. What was it about the structure of the relationship between supply and demand that created the problems? Why did demand overtake supply—the supply of architectural talent, among other things—so dramatically in this country in the mid-sixties? Whose fault was it? Was it just architects, or did it have something to do with the particular way in which we decided to use resources at that time? These are fascinating historical questions about failure and about how so much damage was done. It's not enough to say it was all done by a little gang of Bolshevists who liked white buildings with flat roofs. That's a tiny part of it, but there's much, much, much more to it than that.

Addressing bad design more broadly, Duffy said:

> Bad design is anything that gets in the way of change and attempts to fix what cannot be fixed. I think that's the worst. Then there are all kinds of vulgarities and trivialities that find their way into design, that don't lift the spirit, don't take us any further forward in any way. But I think the rigidity is what I fear most, because it attempts to dominate, to bully nature and people into submission.

Duffy's research and professional work has been devoted to redressing the architectural mistakes of the recent past while looking ahead to the inevitable changes in the built environment. His focus throughout has been on researching user needs and making them the basis for design. Commenting on these goals, Duffy said:

> What I'm always seeking, and it's very hard to achieve, is to design the work environment in such a way that it can mature, that it can get better with time, through appropriation and use—the kind of design that is capable of development. It's very, very hard to find in a world where things are usually designed in a synchronic rather than diachronic way. So a maturing, diachronic design is really what I'd love to see.

3 | Involving Users

Involving users in the design process, simple and logical though it may seem, constitutes a fundamental challenge to most prevailing design methods. As British design historian Andrew King has written, participation has structural *and* political implications for the design process. He notes in the context of one design discipline that

> since the beginnings of industrial design, there has always been a strand of thought questioning the validity of design, in the sense of an activity of elite individuals possessing sole rights to creative thinking. This tradition, handed down from Ruskin to Morris and the Arts and Crafts movement, and even to the early Bauhaus, largely disappeared with the advent of modernism.[1]

Though in recent decades many have discussed the importance of design being responsive to users, few have tried to involve users directly in the design process. Instead, designers have tended simply to make assumptions about what people will like, or sometimes to ask users in advance what their preferences are, or even to present alternative design schemes for them to choose from. In none of these cases, however, are users given a true opportunity to be involved in the actual process of design.

In order for design to be truly responsive, to fully support the activities and aspirations of those who will live with it, it is necessary to involve prospective users in the design process from the outset. One of the few architects to do this is Lucien Kroll. In this chapter, Kroll discusses a number of his projects, emphasizing the philosophy and collaborative methods used in each of them.

Lucien Kroll: Contemporaneous Architecture

Lucien Kroll has, during the course of his four-decade-long career, undertaken a wide range of work in a number of different countries. The common characteristic of all of Kroll's work is his desire, by whatever means necessary, to become intimately involved, before beginning the planning of form, with the communities to be affected by his design work. He has spent most of his career designing urban schemes, housing developments, convents and monasteries, schools, theaters, and the like. Lately, however, one of his primary undertakings has been to help rehabilitate the failed housing schemes of the 1960s, particularly those in France.

Kroll is active not just as an architect and town planner but also as a polemicist for user involvement in the design process. He has lectured and written widely and has also won a number of architectural awards. Among the most recent of these was a second place in the *Chicago Tribune*'s 1993 competition, which focused on the redevelopment of Chicago's troubled Cabrini-Green area.

Portrait of Lucien Kroll.
(Photograph by C. Thomas Mitchell)

Modernism, Postmodernism, and Beyond

Kroll refers to his work as being "contemporaneous," neither part of the modernist past, which is known, nor part of the future, which is completely unknown, but of today, as things are. Though he has written and taught, Kroll's main focus has been on the practice of architecture. When questioned on this, he said:

> As far as I am concerned, going through the whole process of construction as it exists with its qualities and defects is important to avoid the theories, the personal projections, the wishes, the dreams. Even if these are necessities! This guarantees that we are in the contemporaneous reality, not the modern dream. The results are not as ambitious as speculations, but I think they are more authentic.

As these comments indicate, much of Kroll's work is motivated by a strong dislike of the legacy of modern architecture.

> Gropius and Breuer and those at the Bauhaus identified, before the Second World War, mathematical mechanisms in society, culture, and behavior that they called rationalism. They were trying to design what they called the "minimum Existenz" house. This was not the minimum house for existence; it was a horrible joke. But they didn't know that they were joking. The *minimum Existenz Haus* was for them the most logical organization of a family both in a certain time and forever. They called it the "ultimate solution." I'm very rude, but it's exactly parallel to what happened in Germany just a few

(above)
Lucien Kroll, exterior view of Medical Faculty Buildings, Catholic University of Louvain, Woluwé–St. Lambert, Belgium.

(Courtesy Lucien Kroll)

(above right)
Lucien Kroll, interior view of Medical Faculty Buildings, Catholic University of Louvain, Woluwé–St. Lambert, Belgium.

(Courtesy Lucien Kroll)

years afterwards to foreign people and to the Jews. It was the *same*. In every social organization there was a revival of subjectivism—they wanted to be mechanical. That was the way of thinking in that time of the modernists, but that way of thinking hasn't disappeared at all, though sometimes it's hidden behind decoration or lipstick. Now postmodernism, the death of modernism, has liberated us from that, though many architects still dream about being in the twenties because it's something very comfortable for *them*, for their profession—they design buildings that are square, white, cubic, and without any complexity.

Lucien Kroll, elevation of Cabrini-Green "Green Mile" proposal for Chicago, Illinois.

(Courtesy Lucien Kroll)

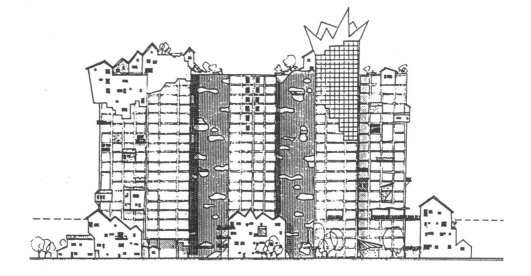

When asked for his view of more recent developments in mainstream architecture, such as postmodernism, Kroll responded:

> I don't know exactly what postmodernism is. For me it's just a matter of the calendar, everything that occurred after modernism died, around 1972, or after Robert Venturi's books. After Venturi we are free suddenly to do any-thing—bad, good, common, any kind of thing. We were not free before. For fifty years we were imprisoned by the modern movement, Walter Gropius and the Bauhaus especially. If I were living in the twenties, I would probably observe something else about the Bauhaus, which was necessary in that moment. But I'm living in the nineties, not in the twenties, and we can see things more clearly.
>
> Though I am aiming my comments especially at Gropius, they probably apply also to Mies van der Rohe's work and to Hilberseimer's schemes of town planning, which are horrible. All of them refuse in their architecture to include any forms that were discovered before. That's exactly the definition of schizophrenia or autism: to separate oneself, out of the deepest anxiety about the outside, from the world and from the closest people around you. I should like to find an urban psychoanalyst to try to dismantle the functional mechanism that suddenly led every architect to be rationalist, to be a modern architect, to be from the then-present day, to forbid himself with a mania near madness to use any form reminiscent of ancient times. That is a deep mental illness. The modern movement was based on that form of mental ill-ness. I'm sure something was deeply wrong there and that postmodernism has liberated us from that illness. Certainly, we have seen also that postmod-ernism itself is nonsense, that it doesn't lead anywhere. But at least we are free to go outside that little world of the modernists.

In his own work, Kroll has focused explicitly on the many factors that affect the success of buildings in use.

> The residents of the projects we work on have already created a psychologi-cal/cultural/social environment, and I try first to understand it and then to

(below left)
Lucien Kroll, Lycée d'Enseignement Professionnel Industriel, Belfort, France.

A house for a teacher at the foot of the social towers. (Courtesy Lucien Kroll)

(below)
Lucien Kroll. Lycée d'Enseignement Professionnel Industriel, Belfort, France.

The roof of Kroll's school, seen between the two towers. (Courtesy Lucien Kroll)

(right)
Lucien Kroll, Lycée d'Enseignement Professionnel Industriel, Belfort, France.

Kroll designed this second-floor passage in the school to "allow physically handicapped people to go everywhere easily in the building."
(Courtesy Lucien Kroll)

(far right)
Lucien Kroll, Lycée d'Enseignement Professionnel Industriel, Belfort, France.

Interior showing the electrical workshop with wooden structure.
(Courtesy Lucien Kroll)

interpret it. We are, however, architects and not social workers. We are trying to give them form not simply by following their popular culture (it does exist, and it is not exactly mine) but by delving into their behavior to check if we are right or wrong, if possibly we see them as they are. I try to imagine that they have something in common—that is, after all, society. They live in a town, they have a human interest in living together, and they behave on a small, human scale. This scale has been forgotten for fifty years. Modern buildings have the scale of the machine or of mathematics, not the scale of human beings, which is a very sensitive and complex thing, reliable from people to people and from race to race also. It is that sort of rich attitude which we try to transform into images and spaces. In the Gennevilliers project in France, for example, we have won a competition based on that.

The Gennevilliers Competition

Describing the Gennevilliers competition, in which an existing housing estate is to be redeveloped, Kroll said:

> The competition was a bit funny because we had to stay alone in our atelier without contacting the inhabitants. We were frustrated by that, and we asked an ethnologist, Arlindo Stefani, to walk around and just describe what he felt about the area. He is not an architect, so he produced a text that helped us not with precise information but with an attitude. He's always positive in these ugly, miserable neighborhoods. He finds them beautiful because he

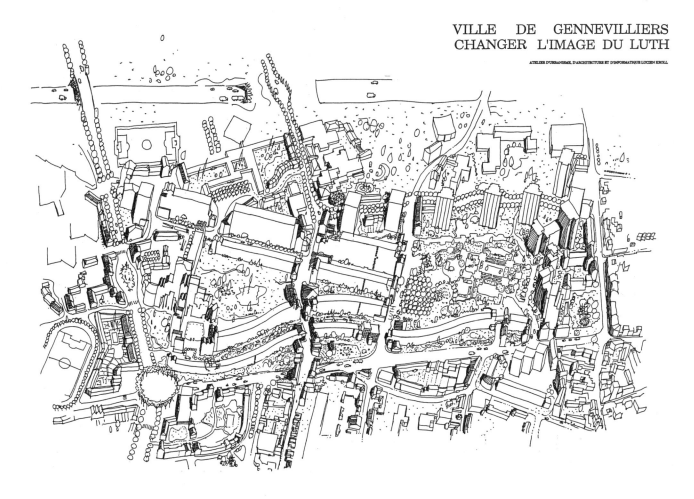

VILLE DE GENNEVILLIERS
CHANGER L'IMAGE DU LUTH

ATELIER D'URBANISME, D'ARCHITECTURE ET D'INFORMATIQUE LUCIEN KROLL

Lucien Kroll, Axonometric of Gennevilliers, France.

Competition entry.
(Courtesy Lucien Kroll)

always sees something human everywhere, the trace of a child, graffiti on the wall, placards and signs, and so on. He says, "Oh, there's someone living here," as reflected by the "ant paths" that pedestrians produce in the lawns, for example. He analyzes the impression made by the real town, not the design of the former town planner or the architect.

On the basis of the ethnologist's report, Kroll's team has created a scenario for replanning the area.

In front of these huge buildings, we imagined a group of pedestrians want-ing to go from south to north, demolishing the prefabricated slabs they encounter. But as they are civilized, they immediately repair and build, according to their own civilization, which is underpinned by complexity, not repetition. There is some disorder, but it results in a street wrapped with buildings, with multiuse facades, with living substance. Pedestrians going from south to north—that was my hypothesis, my fairy tale to begin the process. This would create a street that met all the other streets. The focus of the project is to consider the attitude of each pedestrian going to and fro.

The client has organized meetings, and as it stands now, we will have six evenings with residents of different parts of the neighborhood, which is great. We will discuss everything. I won't propose a project; I will propose a design, a pedagogical image offered considerately, not aggressively, to responsible people, inhabitants, fragile people, low-energy people so that they may follow it or say something to the contrary or justify themselves or propose something else. This will be done in groups, never in isolated discussions. I hope it will produce something interesting. At the moment, they are complaining that they don't have the budget—but that is not the worst thing. They will certainly find in the French organization of the *banlieue,* the city suburbs or outskirts, that the government is desperately trying to avoid what has happened in England and in America—that is, the ghettoization of each neighborhood, with all the poor people together, all the black people together, and so on. I don't know if they will succeed, but getting the atmosphere right is absolutely critical.

When asked if his collaborative processes, such as the one being used at Gennevilliers, involve concrete design proposals or simply suggestions for ways that potential inhabitants can think through the design process, Kroll responded:

It is not enough simply to propose a way to think about design. We present a design that has all the appearances of a complete project. If no one says anything or makes any objection, we may build it as is. But our designs and collaborative processes are so structured that if someone wants to remove such and such a building from here to there, we can agree. The project is done soft, accepting these things. Not silliness, not absurdities, naturally. But in our projects, it is always possible to cope with something based on the attitude of an inhabitant. Let's just say that there are no rigidly parallel lines, so if someone wants to have an oblique one, it's very easy. The designs are not assemblages of regularized units, so if someone wants to let this or that garden be bigger or smaller, it's quite easy. And the more they change, the happier we are. So it's a good direction. Our project has to *seem* to be definitive and you have to explain that they may not move just anything, but on a certain scale, on their own scale, they should change as many things as possible.

The Participatory Design Process

One of the most misunderstood aspects of any project involving collaboration is the extent to which the architect or designer guides the process and determines the latitude given to laypeople in design decision making.

That relationship is difficult to explain. I had a friend who said to me once, "I was really astonished when you spoke about participation, saying that the

inhabitants have authority. That's not true; you're lying. I'm building with cement blocks; you are building with inhabitants."

He was half right. I mean, I still maintain the central authority on everything because my mandate is to manage that authority. My management strategy is to gather people together, listen to them, and interpret what I hear.

In our project in Cergy-Pontoise, however, some people designed their homes exactly, with all the dimensions. We copied precisely the inhabitants' designs, drafting them to the millimeter. Also, everyone there chose their own locations on the site. For instance, we made a bend in a street because one of the inhabitants wanted to live right where the middle of the street was. So that made a curve, which worked out well. We were very satisfied with the outcome. So on some occasions we don't do anything but just copy.

I do, in my work, have one overriding aim, which is to engender a sort of "pedestrian civilization"—I don't know what else to call it. I have tended in that direction and that direction alone. I intensely want to have a richness of relationships readable in the landscape, and that is how I make my design.

(above left)
Lucien Kroll, Cergy-Pontoise, New Town, France.

Here future residents are discussing and working on the plans for the development.
(Courtesy Lucien Kroll)

(above)
Lucien Kroll, Cergy-Pontoise, New Town, France.

View of the site from the village of Vincourt.
(Courtesy Lucien Kroll)

I feel it is also the design of the inhabitants, but until now they have been unable to realize it, draw it, or explain it mechanically. We have a core of common culture somewhere, and that creates the material for town planning or architecture that I need. That means I don't design architecture by "building with inhabitants," as if they were cement blocks. But I'm not neutral, either. At least, I have to go beyond what inhabitants say. If someone proposes something modest or tentative and I enlarge it ten- or a hundredfold, the proportion is no longer what the inhabitant conceived, but he feels at home because it's a good direction, the direction he proposed. It is also compatible with his neighbors, who have approximately the same direction. But it goes far beyond what they would do alone.

The opposite of this process occurred in France, where for years they had an organization, started before the war, called *Castor* [Beavers]. People, very often workers, would get together and decide to build their own houses. The administration in France helped to protect *Castor,* so people were able to borrow money, buy materials, and work without builders. They just made their own houses. And I visited some of them. *Castor* had received an architect's plan from the agency that was helping them. Everyone just built following that plan, without changing anything outside. The result was a repetition, a stupid landscape. With that fantastic organization for collective work, they created something very silly.

I don't produce that—there's no risk.

The Nîmes Rehabilitation

The key to Kroll's collaborative design process is the promotion of a meaningful discussion of architectural and planning issues in terms that the inhabitants can understand. Describing one such case, in application to a social housing rehabilitation project in Nimes, France, Kroll said:

They need more housing in France. There is a shortage. But some of the dwellings in the project we worked on in Nîmes are now uninhabitable.

In this rehabilitation there was a social neighborhood called Valdegour, a scheme with towers and slabs. We had to go very fast, happily, so we designed some things before going to a meeting with the inhabitants, some of whom were very angry. They said that for years and years they were promised everything by the owners who, in the end, didn't do anything. And these very angry people asked us what we were doing, again the same trick?

We had made a model of Nîmes exactly as it is but with the area for Valdegour left empty, and we showed that model. That's always interesting for them; people are curious about a model and want to understand it. This model was small—one square meter for the whole thing. Then I told them, "We've made the pieces of the project moveable so that you may explain what you think about your neighborhood and we can do what you say, or try to do what you say. And the residents said, "Hey, we don't have any expertise in town planning. That's your job. You have the diploma. You're getting paid to do something." They were angry, those thirty or forty people there. One lady grabbed one of the buildings and flung it far away and said, "I'm moving that!" I said, "That's silly. Why? Just to make a gesture? That makes no sense." And that must have made her still more angry, for she replied, "What are you doing here?" "Well," I said, "if you don't have a project, at least you can talk first. And if you don't have anything to say, that's okay. I'll show you mine."

We had a drawing five meters long—a facade, plans, and so on—and they listened to our discussion of that. The architecture we designed for Valdegour was intended to break the regularity, to demolish part of it, to make stair steps instead of right angles, to add houses with pitched roofs above the ones with flat roofs, to cover the tower with a "hat"—a curious hat, unlike anything they had ever seen, I'm sure. But after one hour of such explanations, we wanted to be realistic. We didn't want to dream. Whatever we de-

(above left)
Lucien Kroll, Cergy-Pontoise, New Town, France.

Here is another adaptation to create a separation of the public and private realms. (Courtesy Lucien Kroll)

(above)
Lucien Kroll, Cergy-Pontoise, New Town, France.

Kroll says of this view, taken shortly after the first phase of the development was completed, "It is impossible for a town planner or an architect to design that rooted landscape!" (Courtesy Lucien Kroll)

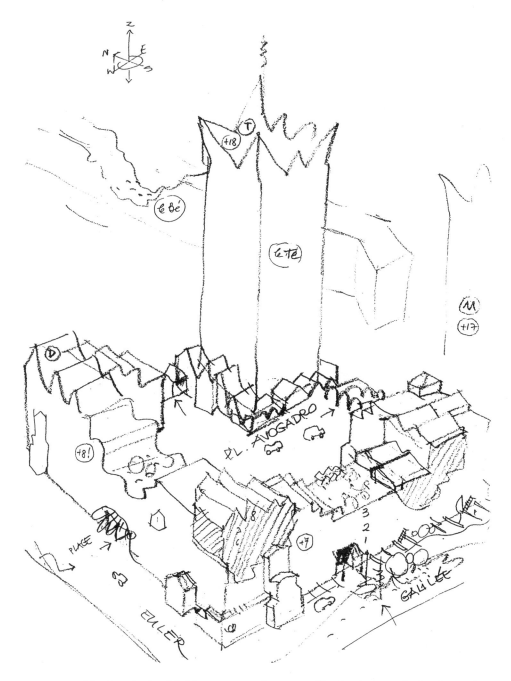

signed had to be buildable at a cost they can afford; I know a little about that, at least. That means that this was a serious job, not just a drawing (and for any architect the drawing we made would have been an insult). But when they saw it, they said, "Yes, that's exactly what we want." Absolutely, without any doubt or any hesitation.

Expanding on the ideas behind the Nîmes rehabilitation, Kroll said:

First, it's a scheme designed to motivate people, all of them—cold or warm, as they say—I mean the government, the inhabitants, the neighbors, everyone involved. It results also in a certain disorder; it's purposely chaotic. There should be activities, workshops, ateliers, shops, places for doing things and

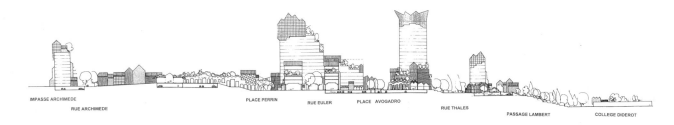

IMPASSE ARCHIMEDE   PLACE PERRIN   RUE EULER   PLACE AVOGADRO   RUE THALES   PASSAGE LAMBERT   COLLEGE DIDEROT
    RUE ARCHIMEDE

seeing things. It's not a commercial center, but there should be a little commercial building, at least. What happens next depends absolutely on getting the people who are interested in being there to participate. Should it be an intellectual worker—say, a liberal architect—who locates there? Or a government agency (which is the case for a little part of it)? Or a post office (which we have in the program)? Each thing should have its own form, should be discussed with real people who know what they want, so that what happens will follow step by step.

Lucien Kroll, Elevation of Nîmes, France, project.

(Courtesy Lucien Kroll)

Ecology and Architecture

In addition to his projects with a social focus, Kroll has been involved in many others that are ecologically oriented. When questioned on the relationship of his approach to the much discussed recent trend of "Green Design," in which attention is paid to the ecological impact of designing, he responded:

All of the environmental considerations should be part of what we try to do, but we have so little information about that, and it's not organized. The consumption of energy, the polluting index, for example, we don't know. We guess and it's dangerous because ancient materials seem always healthier than new ones, which is not rational, but it's a habit. That is one thing, it's a minimum. What seems much more important is that we don't have the image of boxes which have been prefabricated and laid down with the form of the industry, not the form of society. Ecology is much more that: everything should be related to everything else and these relationships should lead to the form, not the process of prefabrication or the logic of having everyone face the south.

Some ecological projects in Holland, for instance, propose identical houses, all with the facade to the south, which destroys the town. That is the military rank, that is not ecology for us, even if it spares energy. Having more sun is agreeable, but we want to avoid the cold organization of one logic. A "chaotic" urban tissue is more ecological than parallel houses toward the sun! So the cross-fertilization of orientation to the sun, trees, shrubs, greenery, interrelated inhabitants, climbing plants—that co-habitation between nature, not as a myth alone, but also as a reality with an impact inside your bedroom, with these things that remind you every minute that you are part of that—that's what we want.

Lucien Kroll, Ecolonia.

Diagrams of patterns for ecological town planning, used in the development of Ecolonia in Alphen-aan-den-Rijn, The Netherlands.
(Courtesy Lucien Kroll)

1
maison
jardin/soleil

eau

2
eau/jardin

maison

3
maison
rue
face avant
verger
maison
jardin

COMPOSANTS

4
lieu central
étroit

porte

jardin/maison/espace central/maison/jardin

5
chaleur ou ouvert
îlot fermé

6
la tour d'observation

maisons/vert

7
passage
étroit

porte

coin

accentuer le passage aux coins

8
deux maisons sous un toit

"villa"

9
toit-jardin

espace
public

eau

maison orientée de trois côtés

10
jardin/maison/rue/canal

habiter le long d'irrigation

chemin/maison/jardin/parc

11
groupe d'espaces fermés

12
porte
/rue

place

lieu central

porte

axe des vélos et des piétons
sur une suite d'espaces différentiés

13
rangée de maisons avec une zone
d'extension spontanée le long de la rue

14
petites maisons avec
espaces extérieurs communs

15
étroit

eau

rue étroite qui
donne sur une "porte"

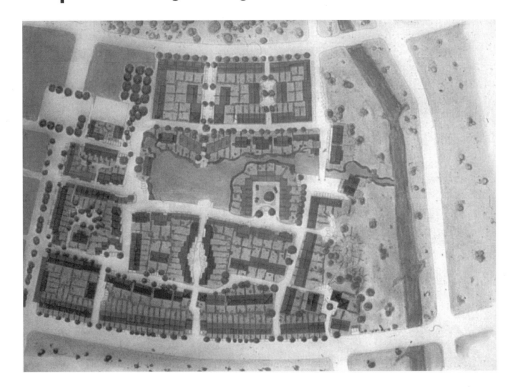

Lucien Kroll, Ecolonia.
Ecological town-planning development in Alphen-aan-den-Rijn, The Netherlands: master plan. (Courtesy Lucien Kroll)

I'm not, for example, a part of the prefabricated scheme in front of my house, but I am part of the ivy on my front wall—politically, empathetically, speaking naturally. So irregularities signify something much more important than do parallel lines, grids, or mathematical forms. Irregularities in volumes are important also, because these little families should show themselves as different families, not the same family, their differences should not be hidden. Similar things? Yes! Identical? No, never! Our work should show that each individual decision is respected.

We had this experience at Alphen-aan-den-Rijn, Holland, in a project titled Ecolonia. We designed 129 community houses, and we asked the client, a social planner, for all of the possible variations—different materials, different colors, different shapes, and different forms of windows and doors

(below left)
Lucien Kroll, Ecolonia, Alphen-aan-den-Rijn, The Netherlands.
The pond with the tallest house in the neighborhood. (Courtesy Lucien Kroll)

(below)
Lucien Kroll, Ecolonia, Alphen-aan-den-Rijn, The Netherlands.
The artificial pond full of spontaneously growing reeds, shortly after completion. (Courtesy Lucien Kroll)

Lucien Kroll, Ecolonia, Alphen-aan-den-Rijn, The Netherlands.

The bridge over the canal linking the pond with an ancient drainage canal. (Courtesy Lucien Kroll)

Lucien Kroll, Ecolonia, Alphen-aan-den-Rijn, The Netherlands.

Houses facing south. (Courtesy Lucien Kroll)

Lucien Kroll, Ecolonia, Alphen-aan-den-Rijn, The Netherlands.

Quay for fishing. (Courtesy Lucien Kroll)

Lucien Kroll, Ecolonia, Alphen-aan-den-Rijn, The Netherlands.

The corner houses at the crossing near the fishing point. (Courtesy Lucien Kroll)

(all of which cost exactly the same price). When houses have these differentiations, even though the floor plans and dimensions are identical, it is not seen as rude or as a political gesture if you repaint your red door in a blue tint because you like blue better. We need people's creativity to help us to do something we like to do. It's contradictory, in a sense we don't help them (though actually we do). Instead we ask the people to help *us*.

Bordeaux Housing Developments

This handing over to laypeople of some of the responsibility for design decision making, relying on their own tacit knowledge and on the knowledge embedded in their surroundings, was perhaps best illustrated by the processes followed in two projects that Kroll and his team undertook in Bordeaux, France.

> Once in Bordeaux, for a project that has not been built, we didn't have any inhabitants so we asked neighbors of the site to come to a meeting in the evening. They were astonished, ten of them came, telling us, "We don't want to leave our apartments. We don't want to go into your new project. So why ask us?" And we had to explain to them that since we are not from the southwest of France, we didn't know the customs, the habits, the way of living there, and we would commit errors or do inappropriate designs. So we should like them to help us by explaining how they live. It's not the same in the southwest and in the north, or elsewhere. Well, they understood. "We want to know," we told them, "how you live. That's the only question: How do you live?"
>
> So they began explaining. They began at something like 8 o'clock and at midnight they were still explaining and explaining. Someone yawned and went to bed, but he came back at 1 o'clock saying, "I didn't speak about colors, so I've come back. I was in my bed, and I was thinking that I forgot something, so I've come back." And there was no end—they were passionate about helping, though there was nothing for them to gain by doing so. Their comments were nothing programmatic, shall we say, nothing precise. But in

(above left)
Lucien Kroll, Ecolonia, Alphen-aan-den-Rijn, The Netherlands.

A group of houses two months after completion.
(Courtesy Lucien Kroll)

(above)
Lucien Kroll, Ecolonia, Alphen-aan-den-Rijn, The Netherlands.

Kroll said of this, "We hoped that some activities could take place in the houses. Spontaneously, a hairdresser has transformed his living room into his hair salon. That's the type of change we forecasted might happen!"
(Courtesy Lucien Kroll)

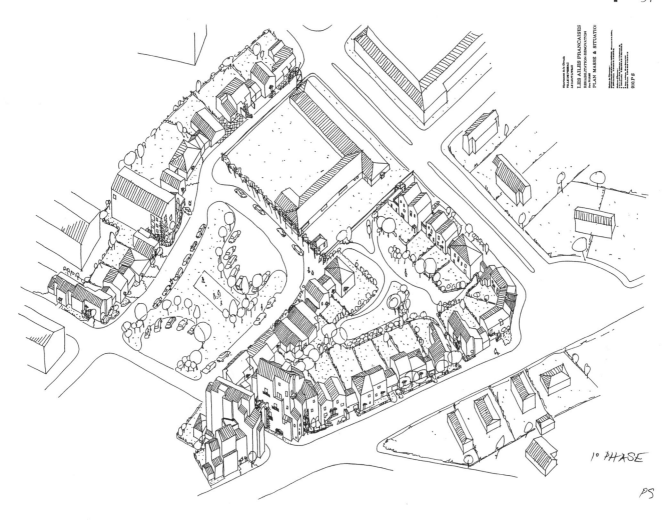

Lucien Kroll, Axonometric of Pessac-Bordeaux, France, housing scheme phase 1.

(Courtesy Lucien Kroll)

a way these people knew each other. They respected each other, and they chatted together in front of us about wine, about what they do on Sundays, about cars, which are important everywhere, especially in the social housing areas. Well, they were quite precious explaining it all to us. I can't say that our design reflected exactly what they said, but at least we had a direction. But, as I said, that project was not built.

We did recently build eighty houses in Pessac-Bordeaux as part of another project, and we are doing a second phase of eighty houses now. We proposed to the client, and he accepted it, to copy the organization of a plan reflecting the spontaneous organization of things built by the inhabitants themselves. That's quite another kind of spatial organization. We proposed a design based on that and some examples are built there. I feel very silly, myself, because it is nearly impossible to design another organization of space inside a house and, as an architect, I am supposed to do that. But we copied something traditional because we cannot invent that.

We may propose anything, naturally, upside down or whatever, but it's always an experiment. It is not intended to be the envelope of a family or a group of families in a certain place and at a certain time. That's an aspect of

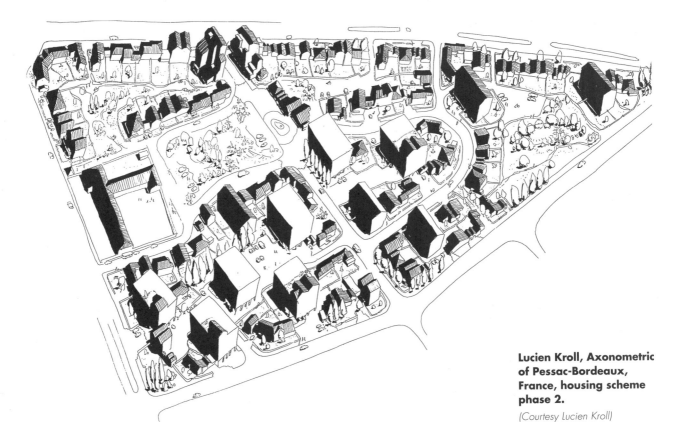

Lucien Kroll, Axonometric of Pessac-Bordeaux, France, housing scheme phase 2.

(Courtesy Lucien Kroll)

participation also, using forms that people are used to. I'm sure that those areas of regularly deployed blocks—the sort produced by modern town planners—don't create the kind of space people are used to, whether it be called a "street" or a "place" or a "crossing." People have known this kind of space in their bodies already for several thousand years. They know it, but the modernists tried to cancel that out.

In this case in Pessac-Bordeaux, I tried to understand as naively as possible that where people walk, that is a street, and that where they stop, that's a place. I also tried to create spaces where people get a sense of orientation through volume, not through x, y, and z coordinates. Ordinary people lose themselves in a grid. Engineers might know exactly where they are, but emotional

(below left)
Lucien Kroll, Les Ailes Françaises, quartier à Pessac-Bordeaux, France: phase 1.

Kroll noted that this illustrated "how we avoid the separation of high and low buildings by creating some of intermediate height to provide continuity."
(Courtesy Lucien Kroll)

(above)
Lucien Kroll, Les Ailes Françaises, quartier à Pessac-Bordeaux, France: phase 1.

This image of the balconies at Pessac-Bordeaux illustrates another of Kroll's key principles; using relatively similar materials, they are all different.
(Courtesy Lucien Kroll)

(above right)
Lucien Kroll, Les Ailes Françaises, quartier à Pessac-Bordeaux, France, phase 2.

This model illustrates Kroll's idea of building maisonnettes on the roofs of the original buildings in the development to add complexity and to change the perceived scale of the modernist blocks.
(Courtesy Lucien Kroll)

(left)
Lucien Kroll, Les Ailes Françaises, quartier à Pessac-Bordeaux, France: phase 1.

Kroll here created row houses that are all subtly different, with complicated garden walls.
(Courtesy Lucien Kroll)

inhabitants don't. Yet they are never lost in an Italian mountain village, which has no precise, geometric form. Topography—that's what we're also looking for inside of buildings. You repeat the street form as corridors, and something like crossings results, especially in larger buildings where you can slow down and chat or sit somewhere. These are motives for doing architecture. Whether a structure is square, round, or of whatever geometry doesn't matter.

Toward a Democratic Architecture

To explain his view of what constitutes bad design, Kroll returns—not surprisingly, perhaps—to his critique of the modernists.

Posing problems and trying to invent a solution to them is the approach that Gropius advocated. That means he imagined it was possible to solve rationally problems that are by definition irrational, that are constantly evolving. For mechanical problems, he's right, even for repairing a car. But for the complexity of the human being or the hypercomplexity of a society, he's destructive. In architecture, it is more rational to be subjective than to be rational.

In contrast to Gropius, I should like to live in an architecture that accords with what I feel people are—and they are not logical. I'm rather rational myself when it's necessary, and the first step in rationality is to stop being rational when it's destructive. Something has to be guessed, this is not naked rationality at all, it's an intuition of where people are. I'm not a philosopher, I'm just an architect trying to understand what are the forms which are populist. I feel it's urgent to know what is positive and what is negative for people—this is the most urgent urban question. But I have no means to know, so I have to bet and to guess and to progress from mistake to mistake.

Describing in more detail some of the consequences of formal decisions on design users, Kroll said:

> In Europe, at least—but I feel in every part of the world—you have two forms of organizations, depending on the nature of authority under which people live. The American grid is a bureaucratic landscape, it's easy to say. It doesn't take into account any natural event, any cultural event, or any topographic event, any river, any mountain, and so on. It's destructive, in a sense. It's a tool, explainable from the point of view of expediency. We have the same, naturally, in ancient Greece or Asia Minor, with grids. Rationally organized space has been artificially imposed on the landscape, and it's the image of the author, and the author is the army. The Roman camp is, by the way, the model for the southwest new towns of the 17th century. These towns are artificialities.
>
> The other tradition is that a natural event, such as the crossing of two paths or of a river and a path, serves as the origin of town planning. Someone comes to do something there, they live there, they build something there—a house or a workshop or a mill. Then right away a second person comes and builds something in conjunction with the first, not as a function of a general layout with axis, symmetry, and so on. Then a third person, a fourth, and so on add to it with a collective instinct. I feel this is the deepest rationality because all the decisions are taken in view of everything that already exists. The very irregular forms of towns which you see in all of the French villages in the mountains or on the plains are a function of the geography. This approach of necessity results in forms which are irregular. I feel this is more democratic than the other approach, which is military.
>
> When architects have power instead of the people, the first thing they do is to impose order in the landscape—everything parallel, north, south, east, west, or a little oblique but not too much—in order that *they* should be happy. That's a minimum, naturally. But this is not the image of people living in the town. They have another form in their guts, in their civilization, in their family, in their history, and in their present also. They are given town planning "off the shelf." I don't feel it's adequate. I feel organic order is more democratic than military order.

The fostering of participation in the design process is an essential precursor to the achievement of a truly democratic architecture. Addressing the nature and benefits of this approach, Kroll noted:

> Letting laypeople participate demands more architectural knowledge, techniques, methods, time, work, and art! In that sense, we have never been frustrated by the inhabitants (when they're in groups and progressing). Suddenly the architect is freer than otherwise. And there is a strange and rare feeling: being useful!

William Wurz, *Pool Computer.*

(Courtesy Michael McCoy)

Mark Stockwell, *Media Blanket.*

This project, by Cranbrook graduate Stockwell, was voted Best of Category in student work in the 1993 ID magazine Annual Design awards. It consists of a twelve-by-five-foot piece of industrial felt incorporating a thin layer of electronic circuitry. The blanket can be adjusted to form an enclosed piece of furniture or opened to serve as a screen for group viewing. (Courtesy Michael McCoy)

Daniel Weil, *Bag Radio.*

AM radio for Apex, Japan, 1983.
(Photograph by Richard Waite, courtesy Pentagram Ltd.)

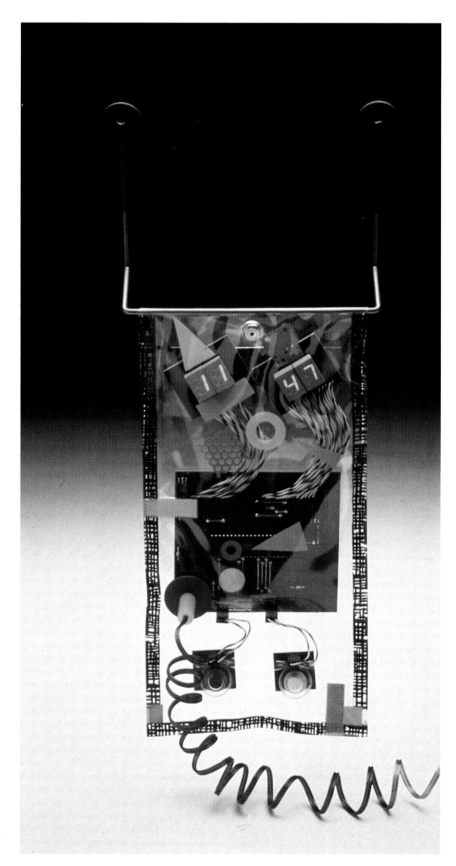

Daniel Weil, *100 Objects: mirrors of silenced time.*

A clock with LED display designed for Parenthesis Limited, London 1983. (Photograph by Richard Waite, courtesy Pentagram Ltd.)

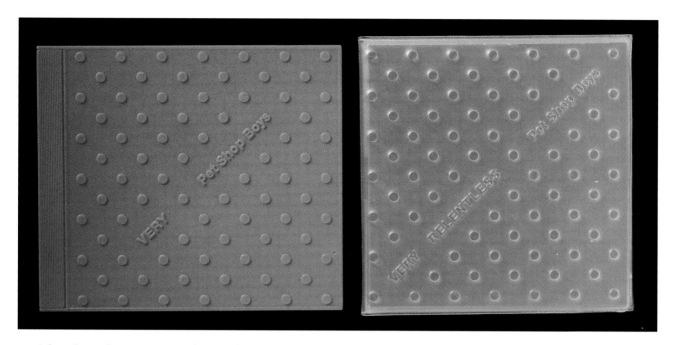

Daniel Weil, market-strategy packaging for the international release by EMI Records of the Pet Shop Boys' new album on 27 September 1993.

The hard-case version is the album Very; *the soft-case is for the limited-edition double album entitled* Very Relentless. *(Photograph by Nick Turner, courtesy Pentagram Ltd.)*

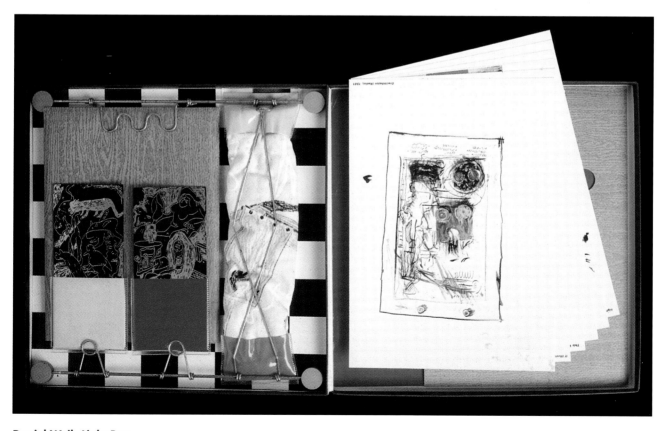

Daniel Weil, *Light Box*.

A publication of the Architectural Association, designed by Daniel Weil. (Photograph by Nick Turner, courtesy Pentagram Ltd.)

DEGW with Knut Holscher, image of Facit iO system.

(Photo: Arne Flink; courtesy Facit Office Furniture, Denmark)

DEGW, model of Broadgate redevelopment.

(Courtesy DEGW)

Lucien Kroll, Lycée d'Enseignement Professionnel Industriel, Belfort, France.

Exterior of the school. (Courtesy Lucien Kroll)

Lucien Kroll, Ecolonia.

Ecological town-planning development in Alphen-aan-den-Rijn, The Netherlands. This model of the project indicates the sites allocated to each of nine different architects involved in the project through use of diagrammatic color. (Courtesy Lucien Kroll)

Lucien Kroll, College Michelet, Saint-Ouen, Paris, France.

The tower of the arts. (Courtesy Lucien Kroll)

Lucien Kroll, College Michelet, Saint-Ouen, Paris, France.

The glazed roof of the school, Kroll notes, is "very loosely designed, without any authoritative geometry, and for the same price as other solutions!"
(Courtesy Lucien Kroll)

Edwin Schlossberg Inc., The Innovation Station at the Henry Ford Museum & Greenfield Village, Dearborn, Michigan.

View of the 3,200-square-foot whimsical "machine," operated by thirty-five visitors at a time in order to create a "dynamic, enjoyable experience." (Photo: Donald Dietz, courtesy ESI)

Edwin Schlossberg Inc., The Money Map System (an Insightguide Project Joint Venture).

An interactive, financial, self-service information system: example of touch screen in the Money Map. (Courtesy ESI)

View of *Image and Object* exhibition organized by DAI at the Pompidou Centre, Paris.

(Courtesy John Thackara)

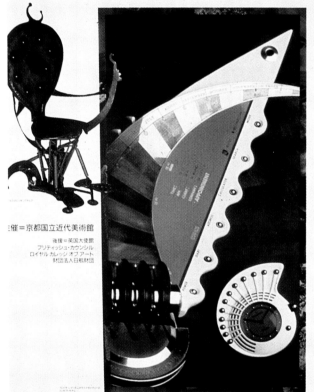

Image and Object exhibition
organized by DAI on tour in Japan.

Video cover. (Courtesy John Thackara)

国際シンポジウム
デザインの挑戦
THE CHALLENGE OF DESIGN

Poster for DAI conference for Asahi Shimbun, Japan.

(Courtesy John Thackara)

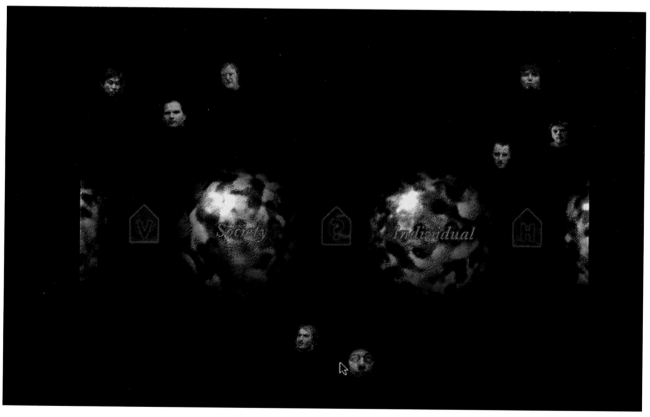

Kristie van Riet and Willem Velthoven with John Thackara, *Doors of Perception 1*— CD Rom (Amsterdam: Mediamatic Interactive Publishing, 1994), home page.

(Courtesy Netherlands Design Institute)

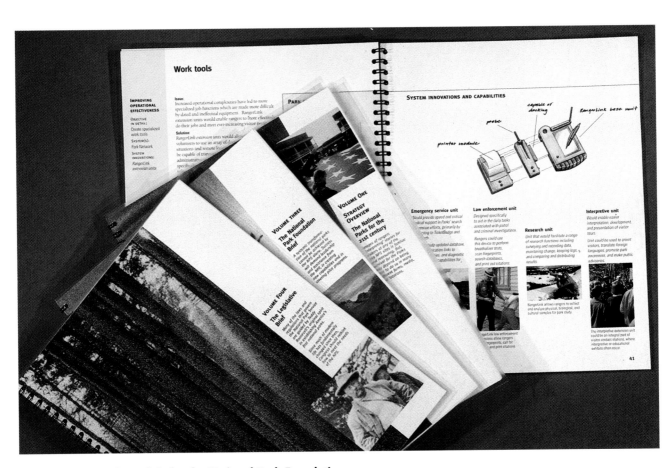

Doblin Group, Design Briefs for the National Park Foundation.

Four volumes setting out a radical new strategy for running America's National Parks. The briefs present a new concept for how the parks could be operated, the types of products and services which might be generated to make them self-sufficient, and the resources and structural changes that would be needed to bring about the proposed transformation. (Photo: Daniel Chichester, courtesy Doblin Group)

4 | Enhancing Perception

Most discussions of design quality focus solely on the formal properties of objects or environments, with the underlying assumption being that aesthetically pleasing arrangements will, of necessity, have a positive effect on those who interact with them. Swiss-French architect Le Corbusier expressed this widely held view when he wrote, "The Architect, by his arrangement of forms, realizes an order which is a pure creation of his spirit; by forms and shapes he affects our senses to an acute degree. . . ."[1] In addition to the formal qualities of space, however, there are many other, more subtle, qualities of environments that affect design users' perception and experience. These more immaterial factors are often overlooked by those who adopt a geometrical focus.

Though an explicit consideration of the subjective factors that affect design users' experience is useful in most contexts, it is critical in application to the design of learning environments, showrooms, exhibitions, zoos, and interfaces. In each of these cases, the very purpose of design is to foster perceptions and inculcate experiences of one type or another. Two designers who have adopted this focus are Clino Trini Castelli and Edwin Schlossberg. This chapter features discussions with Castelli and Schlossberg in which they explain their design philosophies and the work of their firms.

Clino Trini Castelli: Design *Primario*

Clino Trini Castelli is the founder and principal of Castelli Design Milano, a firm whose work explicitly addresses user experience and perception. Most of Castelli's professional activity has involved researching and advising on color trends. In 1973, for example, he established the Centro Design Montefibre with Andrea Branzi and Massimo Morozzi. This project resulted in the Colordinamo, Decorattivo and Fibermatching 25 programs, the last of which was awarded a Compass d'Oro award in 1976. In 1978 Castelli established Colorterminal IVI, the first European workshop for research in color design, and in 1984 he received an IBD Gold Award for his work on color, material, and finishes for furniture company Herman Miller. In addition, he has been a color consultant for a number of automobile companies, including Fiat, Renault, and Mitsubishi. Castelli has also worked on projects for numerous other companies in Europe, Japan, the United States, and Australia.

Portrait of Clino Trini Castelli.

(Courtesy Castelli Design Milano)

Along with his work on color, Castelli has also addressed the role of a number of other "subjective" aspects of space, including light, sound, microclimate, texture, and scent. In 1972 he coined the term *design primario* for this work; a decade later he founded and directed a postgraduate design course on this topic at the Domus Academy in Milan. When asked about the origin of the term *design primario*, Castelli said:

I came up with the term in the seventies when I was obliged to define activities that related to very deep and profound aspects of our perceived reality. The meaning of *primario* is a little bit long, but I will try to express the idea with some examples and metaphors. Something that is *primario* is very subtle in terms of the energy it expresses, but when that level of subtle energy is present at a larger scale, it becomes important. At that point it becomes something very fundamental and strong from the point of view of sensation or communication.

For instance, color is something that in nature is very soft, something with very low energy produced only by the change in frequency of light, something that is not substantial. If I use color in a small way, then the effect is modest; it is not so fundamental. But if I am able to influence the reality of color, as in our artificial environments, in a way that becomes connected with a period such as the eighties or the nineties, then I am able to identify the nature of a certain color in a certain environment in a very large way. For instance, when I work for car companies and recommend colors, you can then see this effect on very large scales; at this point, the low energy of the color itself has become so important that its level of figuration is very strong.

When we work in the design *primario* way we use very subtle effects—in smell, in light, in color, in many manifestations of reality—and we amplify

Clino Trini Castelli, Cassina Showroom, Milan, 1985.

Dome illuminated by gray light. Castelli describes the effect he achieved here as follows: "Whereas most materials reflect light symmetrically, so that the angle of incidence equals the angle of reflection, this new surface is such that light is reflected back along its incident path. In this way rays of light are sent back in all directions from the dome onto the showroom floor, penetrating even beneath furniture, so that no shadow is cast." (Courtesy Castelli Design Milano)

them to a degree that becomes significative at the figurative level—very significative, very expressive, and very important. So this has guided a sort of poetics, a minimalist poetics, that expresses one phenomenon at a low level of energy, at a low intensity, but that becomes very significant when taken on very large scale.

In one case, for example, I worked on a gray-light concept based on retroreflection from a surface, using 3M reflective material. Everyone else uses this kind of material in a smaller way, say, a piece thirty centimeters square on a car or a dress. I did an application on the Fiat Centro di Qualistica in an environment that consisted of two membranes, one of which was four hundred meters square and covered with the material to make it retroreflective. Those who used the space said that when you see the light retroreflected by a membrane of this dimension, you perceive a completely different reality of light. The light has a different geometry and behavior. The lighting of the objects in the space is completely different because you don't have reflections. So the dimension of the phenomena, which is very difficult to perceive and appreciate on a small scale, becomes something fantastic. It is really different—very strong and very significative.

Using a metaphor, I always say that I prefer to work in the dimension that connects my work to *bradisismo*—a tectonic phenomenon similar to an earthquake. *Bradisismo* is a very subtle movement of the earth's crust; you don't perceive any movement, but one day you notice that the level of your coast has completely changed in relation to the sea level. This has happened near Naples and in any area where a bridge or pier is completely different in level from the past. What has happened is that this *bradisismo* movement, though mild, has moved a large area and has had a big effect on the environment, even if it is a small change of, say, one meter. At the other end of the spectrum, you have the earthquake with the manifestation of a volcano that appears in the water in front of the coast. In that case you have a poetic manifestation. If you think in terms of design, it's very strong, very condensed; it has a very pronounced appearance; it is very localized; and it is limited to a certain point. With *bradisismo,* on the other hand, the movement is quite extensive, involving a big area of the crust. I work in the *bradisismo* way mostly.

Metadesign Systems

I have one very important point to make here. Design *primario* is a form of metadesign. It has a meaning only if it is pursued in a metadesign way, if it is a metaproject. So when I talk about color in connection with one simple object, that doesn't have a big meaning. But if I talk about the category of objects behind the single individual design project, in this case it has a certain kind of meaning.

Everybody has experienced the feeling of solving problems connected with a simple object. The real problem comes when you have highly complex products like systems, like the transversal planning of a product line, as in the car industry, or when you enter in the dimension where you have to manage a project completely from zero in terms of immaterial identity. At this point, the metadesign—the ideas behind the design of the single object—becomes significative, becomes very important. By the way, the metadesign makes it possible to do projects that can be used by other designers and applied to any kind of product that follows.

My history in design is entirely connected with metadesign, even my first important professional work in 1969–72, in which I created the Corporate Identity Program for Olivetti. This work resulted in the first manual of a corporate identity to be done in an operational way. It was a metaproject that was done in such a way that you could not solve a single problem finally, but rather so that any kind of problem which resembled the original could be addressed. That was very important and very different. For that reason, I prefer not to work directly on the final object, but with the group of designers who will apply my metadesign system to the single object later. This is very important, this aspect of metadesign, it has characterized all of my activity. I discovered recently, maybe four or five years ago, that all my activity was different from work that other designers have done, and this is very interesting. It now attracts a great deal of attention from universities and from the Domus Academy as it starts to be better understood.

The Qualistic

Though Castelli has been involved in partnerships and collaborations with a number of leading Italian designers such as Ettore Sottsass and Andrea Branzi, he has in his work focused more on the effects of design than on physical form. When asked why he has chosen this approach, Castelli said:

I don't know, exactly. I was educated in formal, traditional three-dimensional design, particularly car design, when I was young. Very soon I started to understand, or better still to feel, that the future of our reality, of our environment, was probably more connected to these kinds of subtle effects that I have gone on to explore through design *primario* than to what we were thinking at the beginning of the seventies. Instead of designing objects like all my colleagues, I started my career designing laminates with glowing lights and things like that. I cannot say exactly why, but to me there was a kind of natural sensibility to that kind of dimension. It was not something that I in any precise way selected, but it was based on a kind of sense that this was important, even if this was not an absolutely well founded belief.

In order to better describe his work, Castelli coined the word *qualistic*.

Qualistic is now in the mainstream Italian vocabulary and is considered an analogy. It implies the perception of quality from a subjective point of view. Quality is by definition—from a philosophical point of view and from a certain point in our history practically starting from Galileo—a quantitative dimension, that is, one associated with quantity. It is a dimension where the perception of quality can be shared in an objective way by any person. So if I talk about color, I talk about the quality of the paint. I say, this paint can resist ten thousand hours of the sun's rays or of ultraviolet light—that is a quantitative quality. But if I talk about a certain type of color you like, you can recognize that this paint has a certain kind of quality. Another person does not recognize any quality in that color, so the qualistic is concerned with the perception of quality connected with the subjective evaluation—it is the perception of quality that changes from person to person. This dimension we have called *qualistic* in order to distinguish it from the quality that has a meaning of quantity and objectivity.

When asked how his focus on the qualistic or subjective side of designing relates to more traditional fields of user research, such as ergonomics and human factors, Castelli responded:

The qualistic has to do with ergonomics and psychology, but it is essentially different because some kinds of human factors are absolutely objective. For instance, if two persons have to use one table I can use ergonomics to do something that will be shared by the two persons. With the qualistic approach I cannot do that. For instance, if one person likes blue and another likes red, I cannot propose a violet that might be an intermediate color to make them both happy. That is very important because it means the qualistic, as distinct from the ergonomic, cannot be shared.

Immaterial Phenomena

As mentioned earlier, Castelli explicitly addresses the immaterial phenomena involved in the design experience—light, color, texture, aroma, microclimate, sound—in his work. When asked how he manipulates each of these qualities and what effects he tries to achieve with them, he said:

> Working with light is the main project of my life because it is fundamental. I am especially interested in the three ways that light is reflected by bodies: scattered reflection, mirrored reflection, and retroreflection, as in the eyes of the cat or in the small drop of water on the top of the leaves in a garden. Retroreflection is the fundamental way to reflect light, and this was never explored in terms of artificial lighting because nobody was putting a large surface of reflective material on the ceiling, for instance. I have now done that. The most recent application, in Japan, was very valid from the point of view of its performance. It was a school for computer instruction that featured three classrooms, each ninety meters square, that worked very beautifully. The reflective material reduced the glare on the computer screens, thus improving human performance for a difficult visual task. This is the main, and perhaps unique, work I have done on light, which I think is something that can be historic and fundamental.
>
> In addition to lighting, there is texture—my passion at the moment. I just completed some experimental furniture for Cappellini International. The pieces are made using a large and different kind of application of texture. This is my actual figurative intent at the moment. I have manipulated aroma in some work presented at the Venice Biennial, but have not developed it further. I have also done some work with microclimate. At the Milan Triennale of six years ago, for example, there was a room free of dust for domestic use. But that, obviously, is a minor kind of thing. I haven't done very much with sound either. The only work I have done was very practical but interesting. It was in application to the control room of a nuclear plant. There was a problem of sound quality, of interpretation of alarm signals and so on. Sound is a field of interest to me, though it is one in which I am less well prepared.

The "High Touch" Office for Herman Miller

In order to more fully set out how he applies his ideas in practice, Castelli focused on the range of work he did in the 1980s for the furniture company Herman Miller.

> I will address my work with Herman Miller from the perspective of today; I'm now working on the office and the nature of the office for the nineties with Olivetti and in Japan with others. When initially I was asked to work for Herman Miller, I saw what the situation was very clearly. If you remember

1981 and 1982, the American office with systems furniture followed a military kind of organization. We transformed this through the Herman Miller project and with the showroom at the Chicago Merchandise Mart for Neocon in 1983. We made it a very "High Touch" kind of environment—introducing a multiplicity of color complexity, as well as other aspects that made the environment very rich, more similar to domestic environment. Or, if you prefer, we transformed the office from a factory environment to a hotel environment, because it is more connected with the public domesticity of the hotel than with the private domesticity of the home.

The aim was to change dramatically the perception of the work or office environment in the world. Today it is to easy to understand that our work for Neocon in 1983 was absolutely revolutionary. Before that time everybody was thinking of the office of the future as an environment that would be very cool, very dry, very futuristic, and very technological. We said, "No, our office in ten years will be like this—a high-touch office with a polychromatic color scheme, very rich fabrics, materials, environmental wallpapers, and wood—lots of rich wood." The feeling of this kind of environment was absolutely different from the others at that time. In fact, offices are still high-touch today. I think it's time to change, right now, but the short-term reality of the office was that one.

As is evident, one of Castelli's primary impetuses in much of his consulting work has been to help "humanize" the impact of technology.

The enhancement of technology in an environment, as in an office where you have more and more machines, is based on a sort of reduction of the sensory stimulation, a limitation of subtle and profound experience. The strategy for Herman Miller in the 1980s was to make the environment more complicated through use of multiple colors, such as the polychromatic schemes, different surface materials used simultaneously, different tactility. All of this was done in order to enrich the environment with light and shadow—to put in more complexity.

Complexity is a humanizing factor in terms of perception. If you are in a single-perception environment, like a red room, it is very straightforward from the point of view of psychophysical reaction. Very soon you don't notice the color; the color disappears because the stimulus is too simple. So the complexity of stimulation is a dimension of humanization, something that reaches people and produces a better condition of life. Nature is complex, and so subtle. We cannot imitate it, obviously, but I think that inclusion of immaterial quality, complexity, and multiple stimulation is a good strategy to balance the aspects of high technology.

Reflecting on his work for Herman Miller, Castelli noted:

It was an important achievement from many points of view. First, because we identified the language of the qualistic of the eighties in advance. I had started work in 1980, and in 1983 we were ready to go to market. Also, in the same year there was the main exhibition of the Memphis collection, so we were able to identify the polychromatic language for certain kinds of spirit just in time. Today this just-in-time nature of design can be realized, thanks to the capacity we now have to analyze this reality, the reality of the qualistic. This is what we think we have contributed in some way through our work: a technique for analyzing this aspect.

When asked to elaborate on this forecasting technique, Castelli said:

We analyze trends with an umbrella diagram based on decades, which I elaborated at the end of the seventies in order to look back and to look into the future. This diagram is something very important for me. We have an arch—the top of the umbrella—that represents historical periods, or decades; then a small arch—the lower ones—representing fashion periods. The latter are contradictory, shorter, but the reference exists. It's very easy now to recognize future trends now in advance. It's easy. We are therefore able to identify what the proper kind of language is for design at any given time.

The Gretel Soft Diagram

Because of his focus on the qualities of an environment instead of its form, Castelli has had to evolve an entirely new design process, along with new methods, to achieve his aims.

We designers presently use a technique that expresses space but not these kinds of immaterial aspects; they are not a major feature of the representations. So this is a very important aspect. If we want to improve the subjective quality of our environment, we have to invent the tools that factor in, or represent, this kind of quality. It's important.

We invented the perspective drawing during the Renaissance in order to express the centrality of man in the humanistic condition. We have today to invent a new kind of perspective tool that represents our condition today. This kind of work involves the drawing many times, so the drawing must be reorganized in some way. This is very interesting and I think exciting, but it's a long process.

In general, in our work we have to use methods because we are talking about what is subjective, aspects that are immaterial, things that are very fragile; we have to communicate the process to other people, and this is part of my effort. Ettore Sottsass thinks that my approach is too scientific. But I, however, say no. I have to survive in a world where I don't talk about poetry or poetics only. I have to create a level of poetics that must be shared by other people, and I have to be very cool from a certain point of view, I have to plan and I have to explain what I'm doing.

Clino Trini Castelli, Gretel Soft Diagram, a "soft" environmental diagram of the plan for the Salon di Palais in the house that Ludwig Wittgenstein designed in 1926 for his sister.

Describing the intention of the soft diagram, Castelli said, "In the diagram we see the irradiation of the heating panels in the floor, the vibration of the color of the surfaces, the diffusion of the rising artificial light, the gust of air forced from the threshold of the two door-windows, and the filtering of natural light." (Courtesy Castelli Design Milano)

The Gretel Soft Diagram is, I think, a beautiful exploration of that. It is really something small, it resulted from an intuition and I did it in maybe a couple of hours in the late 1970s, but I never cultivated it. To me it is not only a way to express diagrammatically energies that are immaterial but also a way to represent a certain kind of world where phenomena happen and have a figuration. To me it is like seeing a space, a drawing, an image.

In fact, I never use the Gretel Soft Diagram, because some time ago I had already begun to think in that way. But every year that I gave the masters' course at the Domus Academy, the first work done by students was to represent their school through an environmental diagram. It was very easy for me to see immediately which kind of people were suitable for the work, whether they were "soft"-oriented people (though I don't like that word) or more objectively oriented people. It was a good test, and this exercise was always given. I have kept many of them. By the way, some of them are beautiful; they express quality beautifully—the qualistic of an environment that until today didn't exist in terms of representation.

I think that perhaps someday or other, someone will start a practice based on such analysis. Maybe it won't be me—I don't know—but I believe that it is something useful and important. Obviously, there will be a kind of common graphic language, such as exists in technical drawing, that will be easier to share. But that is something that belongs to another moment maybe. We have shown a way to solve it; maybe someone in the future will do it.

I myself have intentionally done professional work, not written books, to stress the importance and the urgency of this kind of way of thinking. To test it professionally. Today I've done enough. I'm no longer interested in that aspect of it. But at the time, I was radical in a certain way; I wanted very much to demonstrate that it was something real, urgent, and useful. We have certain strategies in a certain period. In another period maybe they're better abandoned because otherwise we go too deep and lose the total picture.

Return to the Object

Castelli had originally sought to develop the "soft" qualities of design to the exclusion of form. Now he is exploring its "hard" qualities as well.

> I notice that now, because it is twenty years since I began thinking in this way, I am probably ready to change. I have to say that at the moment I am now attracted to the very "hard" aspect, for some reason. But my form has nothing that recalls the traditional formal design process. I have designed furniture but the bookshelves or the chest of drawers that I do express another idea of the form that follows my initial concerns in design *primario*.

Addressing the reintroduction of form to his work, Castelli further explained:

> I know that form was impossible to eliminate, even if the dematerialization of the contemporary technological object is a reality. But now with my clients, such as one that is developing a computer in Japan, I have for the past three or four years, for the nineties, said that the technological object must be rematerialized. I feel that it now reaches maturity in terms of evanescence. In my poetics at the moment, for example in my furniture designs, the quantity of objects is my last concern. But if an object exists we have to abandon the strategy of the seventies and eighties, which tended to dematerialize the object by making it appear very light through color and shape.

Clino Trini Castelli, "Semestri," chest of drawers for Cappellini International.

The piece has twelve "invisible" drawers that open on both sides of the square piece.
(Courtesy Castelli Design Milano)

I think now we have to design objects that are very heavy, very present, very strong in their physicality, because we want fewer objects around us, but those that exist should be very strong. We should avoid producing a lot of very light and very camouflaged ones. This is a very important statement today, I think, and this guided me when I was working on what we have to do in certain fields, like the computer industry in the nineties. Every period is a statement, we must be ready to change strategy continuously. In the last Milan Triennale most people were working on design as concept. I said no, I want to do design again as object, and I want to clarify through form what kind of object it is.

A Moment of Happiness

When asked how he defines good and bad design, Castelli said:

Bad design for me is what I don't appreciate, what I don't notice particularly. The bad things around us are numerous, and they predominate because it is an attitude of man to produce bad things. So bad design is the norm, the dimension where we live. Bad design is the moment where we have no energy, where we think that we are not responsible for something. It's connected with death. When you die you are ready to accept bad design.

Good and bad design have nothing to do with commercial success. We can have fantastic commercial success with bad design. That is normal. So good design is what we hope will remain. Good design has nothing to do with selling a lot or a little of something. It is an effort, a moment of happiness, a happy coincidence of factors. Good design is a real achievement.

Edwin Schlossberg: Creating Conversations

Edwin Schlossberg is the president and principal designer of Edwin Schlossberg Inc. (ESI). He founded the firm in New York in 1977 while designing the Learning Environment for the Brooklyn Children's Museum. Presently Schlossberg and his team of forty undertake a range of activities including master planning, exhibit and environmental design, and the creation of information systems for public spaces and facilities—museums, zoos, entertainment centers and mixed-use developments.

Among ESI's numerous completed projects are The Innovation Station for the Henry Ford Museum in Dearborn, Michigan; The Fernbank Museum of Natural History in Atlanta; The Money Map, an interactive financial-planning system; and Macomber Farm in Framingham, Massachusetts, an interactive working farm.

Schlossberg himself has a diverse, transdisciplinary background, having studied and taught design as well as having earned his master's and doctorate degrees in Science and Literature at Columbia University. In addition to his work with ESI, Schlossberg has written books on a range of topics and also produces "Visual Poetry," a hybrid of text and image.

Portrait of Edwin Schlossberg.

(Photograph by Donald Dietz, courtesy ESI)

Museums and Other Learning Environments

To begin our discussion, I asked Schlossberg if he could explain the ideas behind his work, especially the reasons for his focus on museums and different types of learning environments.

> It's very complicated. The thing that's challenging, interesting, and exciting about doing museum environments is that there's always the opportunity to create a context where people can understand the world more thoroughly and become more excited by it. And also, to create an environment that becomes a tool through which and with which they can explore the world. So the position or the place that I always start from in working on projects is: What can I do to create tools with which people can interact to understand the world better? And what are some of the messages, ideas, and concerns that can be articulated through the experience to engage people and help them see how astonishing the world is, how interesting they are, how interesting what's going on in their head is, as they experience these things? In order to do that, the tools have to be ones that feel as if they're part of a community rather than simply objects sort of hanging in space. By that I mean, the most interesting things we do are a result of a conversation with other people. Sometimes the conversation is sort of a delayed-feedback conversation, where a scientist discovers an idea and we create a context through

(above)
**Edwin Schlossberg Inc.,
view of the Learning
Environment at the
Brooklyn Children's
Museum.**

*(Photograph by Donald Dietz,
courtesy ESI)*

(above right)
**Edwin Schlossberg Inc.,
The Innovation Station at
the Henry Ford Museum
& Greenfield Village,
Dearborn, Michigan.**

*View of the 3,200-square-foot
whimsical "machine," operated
by thirty-five visitors at a time
in order to create a "dynamic,
enjoyable experience."
(Photograph by Donald Dietz,
courtesy ESI)*

which that idea can be communicated so others understand it. Or it can be something where the tool that's in the physical space serves as an experience on the basis of which you can understand the person standing next to you better. The most powerful experiences are ones in which you sort of elbow the person next to you and say, "Did you see that?" or "Can you believe that?" or "I never understood anything like that." So, always my hope is to create tools that enable people to have that kind of interaction and conversation with other people in the space. Every time I design a facility, a difference emerges between the community of people speaking through the museum and the community of visitors; what kind of ideas and things and thoughts and experiences each brings. In other words, the thing that changes the kind of things you design for one facility or another has to do not only with the physical environment but also with the nature of the community using this as a context in which to communicate.

**Edwin Schlossberg Inc.,
Macomber Farm,
Framingham,
Massachusetts:
Sight Masks.**

*These masks allow visitors to
see as different animals do, in
this case as sheep.
(Photograph by Donald Dietz,
courtesy ESI)*

Asked for an example of how he realizes some of these aims in his work, Schlossberg referred to one of the early projects his firm completed, the Macomber Farm, a forty-six-acre model farm and humane-education center for the Massachusetts Society for the Prevention of Cruelty to Animals. The exhibits that ESI created enabled visitors to experience the world from animals' point of view. Addressing the concept for this type of work, he said:

> Well, the thing I like to try to do is to make people unfamiliar with their own behavior, either by doing something unfamiliar or by doing a familiar thing in an unfamiliar way. We invented these masks that let you see the way a horse sees, or a cow or a sheep or a chicken. You put the mask on, and immediately your nervous system tries to look at the world and at the same time model all the cow or horse behaviors that arise from the way they apprehend the visible world. Your nervous system becomes the arena in which discovery happens. You're not just a passive observer to a story line that someone else has created. The thing I always try to do is create experiences that allow learning to happen through your own discovery process. If your "learning experience" is a scenario unfolding according to someone else's outline, you're really just a witness to their discovery.

A similar approach was employed in ESI's recent design for The Fernbank Museum of Natural History in Atlanta. In this case, as Schlossberg noted, the visiting children wore

> both webbed feet and gloves that had screwdrivers or wrenches or other tools at the end of their hands so they could see what adaptation was like. You know that each tool is adapted to function in response to a physical constraint that's in the world.

When asked if he always uses an approach in his work that focuses on user experience, Schlossberg replied:

> Yes, always. That's always the idea: to create those experiences is the focus of my attention and in a certain sense, to get out of the way. I mean the old idea of an artist or a designer was to create something beautiful that people would admire. People would learn more about the artist or more about the object. The thing that I'm much more interested in is to create something where it's a tool which you use, rather than something which you visit: it's more like a microscope than it is a sculpture.

Because these learning environments are by nature dynamic, I was interested to learn if Schlossberg's firm had an ongoing involvement in projects after their initial completion.

> It always continues. My wish is usually that I'm not involved in that; that it continues to evolve with the people who have to live with it all the time. For instance, the Children's Museum in Brooklyn has evolved tremendously

THE MAP OF GEORGIA

TEACHER RANGER PACKS
TEACHERS RECEIVE MAPS, TOOLS AND SUGGESTED LESSONS TO HELP PREPARE FOR CLASS VISITS.

CHILD SCOUT PACKS
CHILDREN RECEIVE SCOUT PACKS CONTAINING TOOLS OF OBSERVATION AND MEASUREMENT TO USE IN THEIR EXPLORATION OF THE MAP OF GEORGIA.

STRUCTURED GROUP ACTIVITIES
CHILDREN CAN PARTICIPATE IN ACTIVITIES SUCH AS GAMES, STORYTELLING AND SEASONALLY RELATED EVENTS.

GIVEAWAYS
CHILDREN ARE GIVEN TOOLS THAT THEY HAVE USED IN THE MAP OF GEORGIA TO USE AT HOME.

THE FANTASY FOREST

SENSORY TOOLS
CHILDREN WEAR DIFFERENT TYPES OF SENSORY TOOLS TO ENHANCE OR LIMIT THEIR HEARING, VISION AND SMELL.

HANDS
CHILDREN USE DIFFERENT TYPES OF ANIMAL HANDS TO INHERIT OR EXTEND THEIR ABILITY TO GRASP, REACH AND CARRY.

SUITS
CHILDREN WEAR ANIMAL SUITS OF DIFFERENT COLORS AND PATTERNS THAT AFFECT THEIR ABILITY TO BE SEEN AND THE KINDS OF BACKGROUNDS THEY CAN HIDE AGAINST.

FEET
CHILDREN PUT ON FEET THAT AFFECT THE WAY THEY WALK AND THE KINDS OF SURFACES THEY CAN WALK ON.

7. Programmatic Tools

Discovery Room Concept
Fernbank Museum of Natural History

©1986 Edwin Schlossberg Inc.
December 22, 1986

Edwin Schlossberg Inc., Fernbank Museum of Natural History, Atlanta, Georgia.

Programmatic tools diagrams.
(Courtesy ESI)

since it was first built. I have gone to see it, and I've noted how it has evolved. And I've given my reaction to what I think has happened—but not in terms of controlling it. Because I think that, inevitably, if I stay with it, people become polite and think not to "get it dirty," not to change it because they think it will offend me. So it's good to step out of the way because we still have this mythical notion about designers that they are more important than the thing that they've designed.

Interface Design

In addition to its environmental design work, ESI has also begun to design interactive information systems that, while necessarily different, share their conceptual underpinnings with the firm's other work. Referring to ESI's Money Map project, for which the firm did the research, design, and production of a system and kiosk for an interactive financial-planning system, Schlossberg noted:

> This is a different kind of activity. But if you know the work of Gregory Bateson (he wrote *Steps to an Ecology of Mind*), you'll recall him saying that to get people involved in a process, you have to make their participation essential for the completion of the task. If they're outside of the loop, then they only become observers to the task. In the computer interactive stuff we do, what I try to do is design it so someone feels as if their cognitive experience with the

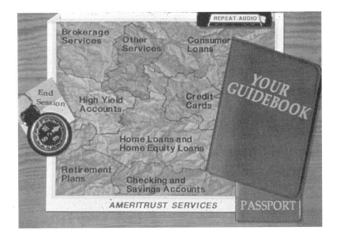 

(above left and right)
Edwin Schlossberg Inc., The Money Map System (an Insightguide Project Joint Venture).

An interactive, financial, self-service information system: touch screens in The Money Map.
(Courtesy ESI)

screen is essential for the ideas of the system to be realized. If you sat down at our Money Map, which is a banking system, I think it feels like we've been waiting for you to come along, we're so happy you sat down and we really need you to participate in this in order for the thing to be alive.

When asked to compare this view of design collaboration and participation to some of the prevailing approaches to these topics in the design literature, he noted:

Well, usually I think that people set it up sort of like they cook the whole meal. They leave one extra chair at the table and invite you to come and sit down. I don't think that's participation. That's just asking someone to join in something you've already figured out. I think participation means you decide together what you're going to eat or what you're going to grow. Then you grow it. Then you figure out together how you're going to cook it. You figure out what you're going to do to prepare it, and you decide who's going to be there when you sit down. Then you eat it and talk about what you got from it. I think participation means that you really accept the fact that your skill lies in suggesting that everybody may need to eat someday. You help express the fact that they're going to want to eat, that they're going to have to anticipate, and that they're going to have to think about the things they'll need for that.

De-Signing

As the types of work that Schlossberg and his firm undertake are so diverse, he consciously avoids labeling, and therefore limiting, them.

The word *design* has always intrigued me because a sign is a label for something, and if you have a label you must be familiar with it. The process of "*de*-signing," of taking the label away, suddenly frees that something from being what it was to become something new. A great design process is one in which something that you're familiar with—you know, a museum or a computer program or a mask or whatever—becomes something new because you've transformed it. That process of transforming it takes it from being a static object to becoming something you can really use. It's nice that the word supports that process.

Similarly, Schlossberg does not consider himself a designer.

I just think that what you are is a label other people put on you. The only thing I call myself is "Edwin"—actually, I didn't name myself Edwin; my parents did. I don't think it's very productive to call yourself anything. You just do what you do, and then people can call you what they like. I like the process I just described that designers do, so I like to do that. But I don't consider myself a designer. If someone else thinks that what I've done is a good design, then they can call me a designer. But I don't like to call myself anything. I like the word *amateur:* someone who loves what they do.

ESI's Design Approach

Because Schlossberg approaches all of his projects with a similar aim, I was curious to learn how he brings about the effects he desires in his work. When asked if he uses a specific design approach on all of his projects, he responded:

You know, I don't. I think the way it happens is a very mysterious process. Usually the thing I know to do when I start on a project is to listen and look very intently at the people with whom I'm working. I try to spend as much time as I can listening to them describe a variety of things. Then, if I can do that enough, I can really drop into the kind of ethos of the project.

I also try to learn as much as I can about the physical constraints and the operational constraints of a facility and then to really imagine myself as the visitor. I think this probably is the method that I always try to maintain. I think of myself as a visitor coming in for the first time, then for the fifteenth time, and I try to test any thought I have against that parameter. For instance, why would I want to come here again, and what am I learning? Why is it exciting? What is it, for example, about the dinosaurs at a natural history museum that makes people want to go back and back again? Are they the physical manifestation of a metaphor? Or again, what is it that really makes people want to do things over and over again? Is that thing that they do over and over again a good thing or a bad thing, and would I advocate it?

So that's what I do. And the iterative process of coming up with a design has to do really with expanding the group of people that work on it. I believe very fundamentally in the fact that the things that I'm involved with require lots of people to make them happen.

The successful realization of ESI's work is dependent as well on the firm's employees, who have expertise in a range of disciplines, including environmental design, architectural planning, conceptual design, graphic design, computer graphic design, interactive systems and software design, video production, game development, and project management. When asked what those who work for him have in common, and how they go about their work, Schlossberg replied:

> The people come with a whole variety of skills. I would say that the most consistent skill or characteristic of people working here is that they mastered something and then switched to another field. I think that that's probably the best training that you can have in the world, to really learn something perfectly well and then not do it, to do something else. What that does is to say you've really understood how to do something and then you've applied that process to a completely unfamiliar thing. The challenge of this company is to come up with a good idea and then keep creating communication pieces that allow that idea to both evolve and stay as interesting when it's actually built in the world as when you first think of it. The company is organized to maintain that process. There's a project manager who stays with the project from the very beginning to the very end. There's a designer or several designers. There's a group of people who are participants in the process and contribute to it both in ideas and in evaluation. And there's a production team, which also starts from the very beginning so that they understand what it is that they need to get built.

Art Activity

In addition to his work with ESI, Schlossberg is active in the arts, particularly through his production of "visual poetry." Addressing the relationship of the two types of work, Schlossberg said:

> I think the work that I do all by myself, which is what the poetry is like, concerns more the sort of ideas that are very difficult to translate into form. Poetry and art usually are stuff—for me, anyway—that I know I want to say, but I'm not exactly sure anyone else will understand it. This is my way of expressing it. It's very important for me to do that, as well as to do the work with the teams here.

Asked how explicitly his design work has been influenced by his involvement with the arts, he said:

> Well, it wasn't conscious in the sense that I said, "You know, I think I ought to model an idea I learned from someone else." One of the difficult, challenging things in life is to realize that everything you learn, including mistakes and successes, becomes the material for the next thing you do. A lot of

people whose work I find beautiful and interesting and challenging—say, Jasper Johns or Robert Rauschenberg or Wallace Stevens or Niels Bohr or Albert Einstein or Virginia Woolf—all those people, whom I admire tremendously, were basically creating their environment and their tools in response to a world that no longer exists. And so it's not usually productive to use the same tools. But the passion—I think one of the main lessons I learned from those people was the passion to explore life and not to let boundaries interfere, not to let the obvious be embarrassing, as well as learning a variety of ideas about experience.

Edwin Schlossberg,
***Through,* an example of "Visual Poetry. "**

(Photograph by Edwin Schlossberg, courtesy ESI)

From Objects to Tools

When asked for his view of what constitutes good and bad design, Schlossberg responded:

> I don't think I would talk that way, but I think that what I would say is that I think the things that are most successful are the ones where people forget that it was designed and are still using it. The things to me that are the worst designs are the ones that are more treated like objects than tools.

5 | Considering Context

As information technology gets more complex, it becomes more and more difficult to make it comprehensible to users. This is a particular problem with the invention of new types of products, for which there is no precedent, because there is then no established, well-understood design language to rely on. To make matters more challenging still, the overriding characteristic of most types of information technology is that the principal manifestation of it is not so much the *object,* for which current industrial design methods are well suited, but *systems* to be used over time. Most mainstream design approaches are still struggling to accommodate this change in orientation.

With all designs, but especially with the introduction of novel technology, it is important to explicitly consider the social, institutional, and cultural context in which they will be used, "embedding" features to support the understandings and actions of individuals and groups in different situations. Three people who have, in different ways, addressed the importance of making new technology comprehensible are Kiyoshi Sakashita, Donald Norman, and John Seely Brown. This chapter features discussions with Sakashita, in which he explains Sharp Corporation's *humanware* and *lifestyle products* concepts; Norman, who addresses his notion of *cognitive engineering* and the nature of his work at Apple Computer; and Brown, who introduces the concept of *user-centering design* and gives examples of how he is applying this idea in his work at Xerox Corporation.

Kiyoshi Sakashita: Humanware Design

Kiyoshi Sakashita is one of the most outspoken people in the Japanese design community on the importance of user responsiveness. After graduating from the Industrial Design Course at Tokyo National University, he joined Sharp Electronics as a staff designer in 1957. Sakashita later spent three years working in the research and marketing section at Sharp's facility in New Jersey, returning to Japan in 1966. In 1973 he established Sharp's Corporate Design Center in Osaka as a forum for comprehensive design work, the first such center in Japanese industry. Presently Sakashita is Executive Director and Group General Manager of the Corporate Design Center as well as a member of Sharp Corporation's Board of Directors.

Sakashita has helped Sharp evolve a unique design and marketing philosophy, which he described in an interview in *Design* magazine.

Portrait of Kiyoshi Sakashita.

(Courtesy Sharp Corporation, Japan)

> A high proportion of Sharp products are exported and in consumer products we are already gearing them closely to specific markets. We don't divide market areas according to the borderlines of the map. We divide our market area according to the culture. It would be better to call our concept "multicultural design" rather than "multinational design."[1]

The key concept driving the development of Sharp's products is *humanware*, which, as Sakashita explained in *The Financial Times*, entails

> the consideration of products in terms of the total environment in which they will be used. We have learned to study and revise our notions about how people live and behave, and design products that are suitable on both a material and psychological level.[2]

I began my interview with Sakashita by asking about the activities of his 200-person team at Sharp's Corporate Design Center, for which he is executive director.

> Our Corporate Design Center is involved in the design of all products supplied by Sharp Corporation. Its activities include all areas, from CI (corporate identity) campaigns to exhibition directions, design, and architecture.

Humanware Design

I was curious about the origin and meaning of the term *humanware*, which Sakashita uses to describe his group's work.

> *Humanware* is a newly coined word without any specific origin. Rather, it is loosely drawn from the common words *hardware* and *software*. When Sharp reorganized its design departments in 1973 to form the Corporate Design

Center, it established humanware design as its future design direction. The basic idea is to gear product design towards people instead of merely designing hardware and software for their own sake. In simple terms, our key design objective is to keep people in mind at all times as the central factor and establish the best possible relationship between humans as users and the hardware/software.

It is evident that the humanware approach differs from a hardware orientation, in which technical capability is the predominant focus of the design process. It was less clear to me how Sharp's approach differed from a software orientation.

Software is designed to maximize the potential of hardware. Humanware is similar in terms of optimizing operability. As just noted, however, humanware can be described as something that strengthens the relationship between people, hardware, and software.

Citing the applicability of the *humanware* concept, Sakashita said:

Current modern equipment has highly complex functions and does not merely work as an extension of human limbs like the simple machines of the past. It is also beginning to incorporate microprocessors and sensors to provide the control and judgment functions that human beings possess. To make it easier for users to understand and operate, modern equipment includes methods to indicate its operation status, not only visually but also by hearing and touch.

It is desirable, wherever possible, for products themselves to provide the user with interactive operating instructions using visual or audible guidance. It's important that something that looks easy to use should also actually be easy to use. I'll specify now some of the ways in which humanware features are incorporated across Sharp's different product lines.

VCR Remote Controls

A visual and audible guidance system is used as an easy program-input method.

(below)
Sharp video tape recorder VC-F300, with remote control.

(Courtesy Sharp Corporation, Japan)

(below right)
Detail of VC-F300 remote control.

(Courtesy Sharp Corporation, Japan)

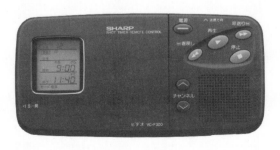

Electronic Organizers

Although the keyboard is integrated into a compact unit, its reaction, feel, and other operability factors are designed to be similar to those of a full-size, desktop computer keyboard. The surface of the keyboard is coated with a mixture of special materials, including collagen, to absorb moisture from the fingers and eliminate any discomfort during operation.

Vacuum Cleaners

To relieve the load on the operator's hands and arms, the vacuum cleaner incorporates an autoreverse-drive motor at the suction inlet to enable effortless operation.

The *humanware* concept described by Sakashita is quite broad and idealistic, so I was interested to learn if there were any engineering constraints that limited the concept in practice.

Production engineering is advancing day by day. It is only a slight exaggeration to say that we can now theoretically manufacture almost anything. It is therefore important for us to focus attention on what to make rather than how to make it.

(below left)
Sharp Electronic Organizer.
(Courtesy Sharp Corporation, Japan)

(below)
Sharp Vacuum Cleaner EC-L5PX.
(Courtesy Sharp Corporation, Japan)

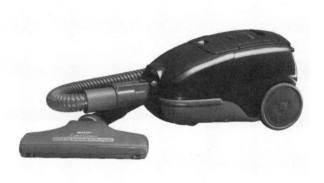

Lifestyle Products

One of Sharp's stated aims is to create a "design that highlights essential values, making the 'aim of a product' and its 'features' stand out for their usefulness in creation of a new lifestyle."[3] When asked about the relationship of the *lifestyle product* and *humanware* concepts, Sakashita replied:

A lifestyle product design is based on the realities of users' everyday lives. Basically, the concept is the same as humanware design, with its focus on people. It is important to remember that human lifestyles vary greatly between regions, races, religions, climates, ages, family compositions, and so on. Our basic strategy is to respond efficiently to different users' requirements under the fundamental constraints of mass production. Although no specific market research method has been established, Sharp's sales network always feeds back users' requests and comments, and they are reflected in the product planning. Here are some examples of this.

Copiers

Large copiers for business use are designed to provide system coordination by taking into account the shape, color, size, and other factors of other office-automation equipment to be used in the same work place. The design of compact copiers for personal use, meanwhile, is coordinated with that of word processors, typewriters, personal computers, and other desktop equipment.

Refrigerators, Air Conditioners, and Microwave Ovens

Refrigerators and air conditioners are designed according to the installation location in the home, for example, as large facilities or compact equipment. Similarly, large and compact models of microwave ovens differ in their design.

One of the ways in which Sakashita promotes an awareness of different lifestyles and cultures is by sending his Japanese designers to work in Sharp's U.S. and European studios.

I consider that the best way to implement designs based on lifestyles is to have those who are familiar with lifestyles in the respective markets participate in the design processes. The resulting products vary widely not only in styling but also in specifications, performance, prices, and so on.

I asked Sakashita whether he thought all products should be segmented by the lifestyle or cultural groups for which they are intended, or if he felt there was a role for some globalized products.

Products closely related to lifestyles such as cooking equipment, washing machines, and refrigerators need to be segmented according to their target market. However, globally standardized specifications are possible for electronic calculators, compact radios, audio products, and so on.

The Design Process at Sharp

I was interested to learn more about the design processes Sakashita and his team use. In particular, I wanted to find out how projects at Sharp are initiated and carried out.

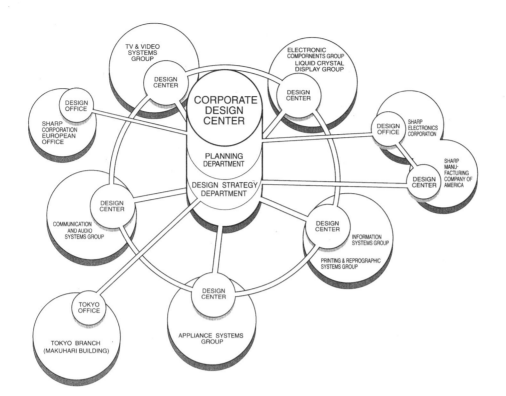

Sharp's Design Organization.

(Courtesy Sharp Corporation, Japan)

Design processes are the responsibility of each design team leader and all members of upper corporate management. There is no fixed person responsible for initiating a product concept. This is done according to normal Japanese corporate practice—by consensus among all the staff involved (that is, the product planners, engineers, researchers and designers). The general direction is decided by group discussion, generally by personnel who have completed specialized courses at high school, college, or university. Education and training after joining the company are also very important for these personnel.

Our product planning departments regard the ideas of the marketing departments and marketing data as very important. The departmental leaders are responsible for the functions and quality of a product. The production engineers make their final decision on the direction of a product from a technical viewpoint, while management does so on the basis of corporate strategies.

In a lecture he gave, Sakashita expanded on this approach:

Recently, a new technique called concurrent engineering (simultaneous development design), or *kurumaza kaihatsu,* has gained the attention of industry. Some people liken it to "coordinated development in which personnel from all departments begin working simultaneously on a project." Several years ago, Sharp adopted the concept of concurrent engineering in its product development. It is no exaggeration to say that our recent hit products, exemplified by the ViewCAM LCD camcorder and the Eco-Awash full-auto washing machine, are the results of this development system.[4]

Essential Design

Sakashita has said that, in his view, Japanese design lacks a strong identity compared, for example, to European design. When questioned on this, he said:

> Japanese designers value teamwork with other specialists more than individual artistic freedom. This may result in designs that lack originality, but it is our objective to design appliances that are useful in everyday life, not to create works of art. Though originality may not always be a prerequisite in a product, I do believe that a Japanese identity is essential in every product.

Addressing design more globally, Sakashita has discussed the transition from "substance to sensibility, from concentration to decentralization, . . . from economic to cultural values."[5] I asked him if the humanware ethic is part of the broader shift in world view taking place in other fields, to which he replied:

Sharp's "Essential Design" concept.

(Courtesy Sharp Corporation, Japan)

> I believe it is also important for us to respond to the changing times, as long as we focus our attention on humanity. What I seek is "happiness for every being on earth through well-balanced design."

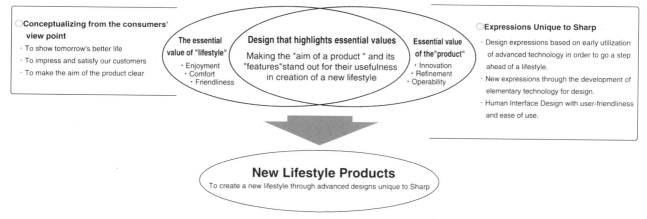

ESSENTIAL DESIGN

○**Conceptualizing from the consumers' view point**
· To show tomorrow's better life
· To impress and satisfy our customers
· To make the aim of the product clear

The essential value of "lifestyle"
· Enjoyment
· Comfort
· Friendliness

Design that highlights essential values
Making the "aim of a product " and its "features"stand out for their usefulness in creation of a new lifestyle

Essential value of the"product"
· Innovation
· Refinement
· Operability

○**Expressions Unique to Sharp**
· Design expressions based on early utilization of advanced technology in order to go a step ahead of a lifestyle.
· New expressions through the development of elementary technology for design.
· Human Interface Design with user-friendliness and ease of use.

New Lifestyle Products
To create a new lifestyle through advanced designs unique to Sharp

Donald Norman: Cognitive Engineering

Donald Norman, unlike most others in this book, is not, strictly speaking, a designer. He has degrees in electrical engineering from MIT (B.S.) and the University of Pennsylvania (M.S.), as well as a doctorate in psychology, also from Penn. Norman spent over three decades in academia, where he was extremely influential, authoring or co-authoring ten books and numerous journal articles. He also became a Fellow of the American Academy of Arts and Sciences, the American Psychological Society, and the American Association for the Advancement of Science.

Norman was particularly important in the development of the field of cognitive science. He has written widely on the topic and was one of the founders of the Cognitive Science Society, which he chaired. He also has served as editor of that organization's journal, *Cognitive Science*. In 1978 Norman left his post as Chair of the Department of Psychology at the University of California, San Diego, to head the university's newly formed Department of Cognitive Science.

In addition to his academic work, Norman has served as a consultant to numerous companies on matters such as the design of user-responsive computer interfaces and consumer products. This interest in the psychological effects of design is the subject of a series of books he wrote, which includes the influential volume *The Psychology of Everyday Things* (published in paperback as *The Design of Everyday Things*). Norman took this interest one step further in 1993, leaving his full-time academic post to accept the job of Apple Fellow at Apple Computer. Since his arrival at Apple he has also been made Vice President of Advanced Technology, which places him in charge of the company's research program. The focus of his work is to define the next generation of computer, which Apple calls the *third paradigm*.

Portrait of Donald Norman.

(Courtesy Apple Computer)

I began by asking Norman to compare his job at Apple with his earlier work as an academic.

> The work I'm doing at Apple differs dramatically from that which I was doing as an academic. A good deal of it is voluntary on my part. I was at the University of California, San Diego, for twenty-seven years and at Harvard for five years before that (I was surprised to discover how long when I added it up). I had been in the research laboratory for a very long time. Now I wanted to experience a very different environment, that of the product side of industry.
>
> I made this transition because I decided that I really wanted to understand what it was like to put out products. So rather than working with the research side and developing methods for discovering, say, what the needs of people were and how to develop new products to address them, I jumped right into the middle of the product world. I wandered about Apple, tried to understand what was going on, visited a majority of the work groups in all parts of the company, and visited the research activity (at that time we had research units at Cupertino, California; Los Angeles, California; Cambridge, Massachusetts; Paris; and Singapore). In looking over our products, I discovered many problems and inconsistencies across the line. I also discovered many groups working at cross purposes within Apple. This is true of any large company, and my ability to wander around the company allowed me to notice things that other people had not. Apple is also a rapidly changing company; it's now moving into consumer electronics—it is no longer just a computer company.

The Organizational Context of Design

One thing I soon discovered at Apple is that although I had spent my life developing the science and technology of good design, that seems to be of secondary importance in actual life. What is much more important is the organizational structure of the company. It doesn't do any good to have the world's best designers if they are in different parts of the company, or if they're called into the process too late to make a change, or if the components required to make a product come from several different parts of the company that report to different executive officers. I discovered this is true not only of Apple but of companies across the world. Most companies are organized according to a hierarchy with separate divisions and separate reporting lines. This organizational structure makes for easy and efficient vertical communication. It makes it easy to keep good financial records, so the accountants love it. It is also good if you want to be promoted because there's an obvious ladder for promotion. But it is a very bad way to do design work because any product really requires assistance and coordinated work from across the company, which means horizontally. But in a hierarchy the communication lines are efficient vertically, not horizontally. So at Apple I'm hard at work trying to invent organizational schemes that overcome this particular problem.

Our industrial design group has had extremely good success in overcoming this inherent organizational limitation by being in one central group located fairly high in the company. They assign one person to each product team and then draw in whatever talent is required from the central team. So this is sort of a cross-organizational structural procedure. This turns out to be an excellent way to overcome the barriers of the hierarchical organization. I've been studying other organizational methods that can improve the design process. In other words, much to my surprise I discovered that although my goal was to apply technology, I ended up working more on appropriate organizational methods than on technological problems.

I commented that there is very little discussion of this issue in the design press, to which Norman replied:

That's true. This is hardly talked about in the design literature. But notice what *is* talked about. Designers, whether industrial design, architectural, product design, human factors design, uniformly complain that they are ignored, that they are called in too late, that people complain when they make suggestions because it will cost too much money or will slow up delivery of the product. It seems to me that designers are not applying their own methods to their own problems, that when you find a problem you ought to step back and try to see what the causes are. If for years designers are complaining that they are ignored, well, maybe there's a reason why. That's what I have been doing, stepping back and trying to understand the problems.

Having done so, I find several problems. One is that the organizational structure is inappropriate, so designers are often thought of as the people you call in at the very end to make the product look pretty or maybe to fix up this little problem with usability. That's the wrong way to do it. But what's the solution? The solution isn't to sort of bang on the tables and say, "You're ignoring me." The solution is to understand the practical organizational problems that led to this division and to develop an organizational structure that overcomes them.

Product people complain that designers only delay the schedule and cost more money. I believe that complaint is correct. And so the designers also have to change their methods so they can produce usable, attractive designs much more quickly. Now part of this change does involve getting into the design process really early, before any major costs are incurred. That requires a good deal of planning. That's, for example, what our industrial design team at Apple does very well: they make sure that everybody knows about their work. They give presentations all over the place, they demonstrate their products, and they make sure they're involved in the very beginning of the discussion of a possible new product. They also have a rule among themselves, "We will never delay any product." If that means their design must suffer in order to meet the schedule, they will allow it to suffer, because as soon as they start delaying a product, other people will start hesitating to call upon them.

It's much more important occasionally to let an inferior design out of the door than to be thought of as somebody who slows up the process. In the field of usability studies, we have to develop methods that respond more quickly. Industrial designers know how to whip up a prototype out of foam or plastic or cardboard overnight, if need be. The people in usability studies can take months to come up with answers. We should all be willing to come up with answers overnight, and we should be willing to have them be wrong. They don't have to be perfect because almost anything we come up with, no matter how quickly, is bound to be better than what the engineers would come up with without background or experience in this type of design issue.

I was interested to learn more about Norman's impressions of the design process at Apple, particularly about how new products are conceptualized and realized.

The design process at Apple is complex, and although there are all kinds of documents that set out the written standards and the process by which they are to be achieved, in fact the process is somewhat different for every new product. But let me emphasize that Apple is one of the companies at which design is taken most seriously and where it is most successful. The problems I see are almost always the result of individuals each trying to do their very best, but seeing the world differently than the design community, or perhaps seeing it only from their narrow perspective and not from a broader, companywide perspective. Much of the bad design we have in the world results from the fact that product team managers, for example, are promoted if they are successful in getting products out on schedule and under budget. Anything that interferes with this is apt to cause them to suffer in their promotion cycle.

One point I like to make is that if, say, the design team could spend an extra six months and an extra, say, half million dollars, they might come up with a design that was easier to manufacture and sell more, which would be overall better for the company. But in fact the design leader would be punished, not rewarded, for this: they took too much time and went over their budget. They're evaluated by their superiors on simply how well they do their part of the job. Furthermore, it's very rare for anybody to sit back a year or so later and look at the success of a product and say, "Gee, that was the result of this one person courageously taking more time and more money than we allowed." This attitude has to change if we really expect to have good design. We have to change the reward structure, and also maybe the reporting structure of design within the company. That's what I've been focusing on most heavily.

Explaining the process currently used at Apple, Norman said:

In part, what happens is usually some technologist or somebody in marketing says, "We need a product that matches our competition, so add the following features . . ." Or a technologist says, "We could attach a camera to the computer and offer video conferencing." Quickly a team of technological specialists is put together. They combine with marketing to do a quick study and analysis of the potential market acceptance of the idea. They do an analysis of the cost of development and manufacturing, they make a proposal to their management, and if it's accepted they get a budget, a design team, and a schedule. By this time, it is already too late for good industrial and behavioral design. Sure, there are usually check boxes to make sure you've done user studies, to make sure that industrial design is involved. But check boxes don't guarantee the intimate, day-to-day involvement with the product that is necessary for success. And at the moment, the only reason that the process works well at Apple is because there are good relationships so that the industrial designers and the user specialists can actually send someone to live with the team. We have some misses as well as hits, and we have to change that. But we're a lot better than other companies I've looked at.

Cognitive Aspects of Design

Though Norman was one of the pioneers of the field of cognitive science, he has more recently referred to his approach as *cognitive engineering*. I asked him to compare these approaches and to comment on their relationship with more established disciplines such as human factors and ergonomics.

I consider cognitive engineering the applied side of cognitive science. The term *engineering* is used mainly to emphasize the application, the practical side. The idea is to take what has been learned from cognitive science and try to apply this to the real world of industry and of products. The term *cognitive engineering* is related to the work done in human factors and in ergonomics. The term is, however, designed to emphasize the cognitive aspects of this area. Traditional human factors and ergonomics have focused on the physical side of the problem, on fitting the design to the body. What I'm concerned with is fitting the design to the mind. In fact, in Europe this approach is often called *cognitive ergonomics,* which in many ways is a better term than cognitive engineering. I think that both of these areas, cognitive ergonomics or cognitive engineering, should be thought of as subdisciplines of human factors or ergonomics. And in some sense, the name of the discipline is an advertisement and an inducement to the field to pay much more attention to the cognitive, mental side of products. But I see this as supportive of the work that is done in human factors and ergonomics.

In his books Norman has gone into detail on many of the psychological principles that underlie people's interactions with design. I asked him to briefly explain some of the principles he identifies, such as visibility, affordances, mappings, and conceptual models and feedback, in terms of their relevance for design.

Visibility

The main point about visibility is not that it's visual or graphical; the important point is that it is permanent. The problem with spoken words is that the words disappear as they are uttered—and you can only remember their content in your memory and working memory is very limited. If I mark a piece of paper, that mark stays there and I can retrieve it simply by directing my eyes to the piece of paper. The visual world also allows for two- and three-dimensional representations, which gives us room for a tremendous amount of information. In the room where I'm sitting, I have objects scattered throughout the room. I know where they are because I put them there myself; they're functionally located. And to remember any given item, I can simply look to the place where it is stored and there it is, and I can now remember its function. So the real, critical thing is not that it's visible—that's an accident of our sensory system—but that it's readily available and permanent.

Affordances

Regarding affordances, the visual cues through which we come to an understanding of how to interact with our environment, Norman said:

The critical thing is not the real affordances but the *perceived* affordances. The problem is: we have to know which operation we can perform and which is appropriate. Therefore, it is important that this information be perceptually available at the time of the decision. Sometimes the designer may want to introduce false affordances, perceptually false affordances, in order to control behavior appropriately. For instance, you may want to make a stair banister look like you could not sit on it. I have seen window sills in stores that deliberately have uncomfortable ridges on them to keep people from sitting in the store windows. I've also seen rubber obstacles blocking a path or a road, and because they look like they're formidable obstacles, automobiles tend to avoid them and to stay off the road whereas service vehicles can just drive over them with impunity because, being rubber, their affordances are false. It is perceptual affordance that governs most people's behavior.

Mappings

One of the major problems in design is understanding the relationship between the actions and results. If you have a perceivable mapping, what I called *natural* mapping, then you don't even have to label the controls. This will work well only if there's a well-known convention or a spatial relationship. You can move something up to make it brighter or louder, but moving it up to make it redder doesn't make any sense. Color doesn't map to spatial direction. Loudness and brightness do.

In controlling lights, which is one of my favorite examples, I point out it's often difficult to know which light switch controls which light, but it's easy to see why the problem exists—it's a mapping problem. Light switches are almost always arranged on the wall in a single line. The lights themselves are almost always arranged in two dimensions horizontally throughout a room, therefore the light switches should also be arranged in two dimensions horizontally with the light switches in the same location as the lights they control. The same with stove top controls. The four burners are controlled by four controls. Burners are usually arranged in a rectangle, so also should be the controls. When you have natural mapping, labels are no longer necessary, and you discover the number of errors people make is reduced dramatically.

Conceptual Models and Feedback

It's very important for designs to have a good conceptual model that is explicitly represented to the user. I call this the *system image*. This makes it easier for people to understand what they're doing. It makes it easier to learn complex systems if you think you understand what is going on.

It's also critically important that whenever you perform an operation, you get feedback so that you know that the operation has been received, even if you can't yet see the result. So it's important for designers to add feedback. Most good telephone designers are careful to feed back the dial tone signals—called the *DTMF,* or *dial tone multiple frequency signals*—so that when you push a button on the telephone, you hear the tone being sent over the wire and you know that something is happening. If you've ever used a telephone where the designer has neglected to do this, you discover how frustrating it is; you don't really know the button push has been received by the equipment. Appropriate feedback makes a dramatic difference in the quality of use.

It's well known with computers as well that you need to tell people, "Yes, I got your instruction. It's going to take me a while. I'm working." This is the purpose of the hourglass or watch icon. On one occasion I tried giving an instruction to a computer system and nothing happened, so I finally decided that the computer system must not have responded, and I restarted it. Then later on I discovered that, no, it had been working away on the instruction. It took a little time, about a minute; but it just never bothered to tell me it was responding.

Affordances for Information Technology

Norman has addressed thoroughly in his books the failure of affordances in many common designs, but I was particularly interested to learn how the concept might be applied to the design of microchip-based equipment such as computers for which there is no physical precedent.

I have three answers to that question. The first answer is to develop "soft" affordances. The second answer is to change the entire structure of computers—in fact, I would like to get rid of computers. And the third answer is to recognize that technologies themselves have affordances and therefore limit or support different types of activities. Let me expand on these answers a little.

In information technology many affordances are "soft" because information is invisible and the working parts of computers are invisible; therefore, the form is completely arbitrary and is left up to the designer. It's not like a door, where there is a physical device—some part that you push or pull—that automatically causes the designer to figure out how to make a perceptual affordance that is easily "pushable" or "graspable." With the computer it's completely up to the designer's imagination. It's a challenge to the designer to create an appropriate system image, to create such a good conceptual model that the user will say, "Ah! I see what the possibilities are" and know immediately how to do things. But it is rather arbitrary. Do you draw a picture of a door handle on a screen? It's not graspable like a real door handle.

In screen design we have developed conventions. There are "windows" and "scroll bars." A scroll bar usually runs vertically and has a darker region with an inner square that moves up and down. The inner square is marked in some way so as to be visible. You either click and drag the inner square up and down with a pointing device, or you click on directional arrows at the ends of the scroll bar to get the same result. These are "soft" affordances. Now, these are very artificial conventions, but nonetheless they offer a kind of affordances of operation. One of my former students, Bill Gaver, who's now at the Royal College of Art (London), has written a paper on technological affordances and tried to explore the variety of technologies and design standards that we develop to make these affordances visible. I think on the whole, though, that these affordances always will be less satisfactory than the physical affordances that we find in the real world, primarily because they're all arbitrary, conceptual, and require some learning and the establishment of arbitrary conventions.

The second answer to the question is itself a question: Why do we have to have all of our operations done through this one box called the computer that sits and occupies an increasingly large amount of space on our desktop? I think the challenge of designing "soft" affordances in part results from the fact that we try to map all the tasks of the world onto this one structure, the computer screen with the keyboard and some kind of simple pointing or writing device. Many tasks are just inappropriately described this way. I think we should devise specialized tools that fit the task and that can actually be physically different from one another. If you wish to draw, you should have a drawing tablet with a variety of different pens. If you wish to balance your checkbook, you should have a checkbooklike device that you can write on or type on and that either spits out a printed check or sends an electronic signal to the bank or to the merchant for whom you're writing the check. If our devices were designed to be task-specific, we could get around the limitations of our contemporary computer, which tries to be all things to all people. Instead, the physical structure could advertise the appropriate affordances.

The third answer concerns the use of technological affordance, which is a very, very different notion. The idea here is that technologies themselves have affordances. The telephone over which we are doing this interview is one. It affords rapid and easy auditory communication, but it does not afford visibility or permanence—I can't see you, you can't see me. On some telephone calls, if we are bored by the conversation, we can read the newspaper, we can wander about the house, we can do all sorts of extraneous activities that would be impolite if we were in front of the person with whom we were conversing. But they are possible on the telephone because they do not have the affordance of visibility. Because a telephone conversation is conducted entirely by voice, it doesn't afford memory. And it's this lack of affordances of a telephone call that actually leads to a number of difficulties or restrictions of our capabilities.

In my book *Things That Make Us Smart* I go through the affordances of technologies. I point out that because different technologies have different affordances, they can't be used for some kinds of tasks, but they're especially well suited for other kinds of tasks. Many of the problems we have with technology today result from the fact that we take a task for which a technology is not well suited and we try to force it. The voice-answering systems that are so prevalent in business today are a good example of this. When you call a business with a question you're apt to be greeted with a voice-messaging system to direct you to just the one place where the information you seek is available. But since there may be thousands of possible places, you must be given a set of alternatives. People are, however, only capable of remembering about three options auditorially presented at one time. So there's a problem: if you can only give three or four choices at any moment but you've got to direct the person to one of many thousands of options, the path is going to be long and torturous as well as highly susceptible to error and frustration. I think these voice-messaging systems are trying to fill a very important need, and they can be valuable to both sides of the conversation, but not with today's technology. With today's technology all they do is frustrate the caller. There's no solution if you stick to voice telephones, by the way; it's not a matter of redesigning the voice system. I think the only solution is to change the affordance of the technology, which means adding visual screens and displays to telephones.

Given his background in cognitive science and his present employment by Apple Computer, Norman's second response, his call to get rid of the computer, was particularly ingriguing. I asked him to expand upon this point.

I think computers today are in a horrible state. We have all the sins of the old-fashioned mainframes sitting on our desks. They're getting much too complicated, much too difficult to use. We're trying to map every task known onto a simple keyboard and pointing device and computer screen. It was easier in the old days, when they were simpler and could do limited tasks. I believe in the future, when they're so powerful that you don't even have to see them, they will become embedded in our devices. I have a very old issue of the Sears Roebuck catalog, issued around the turn of the century, in the early 1900s. They were advertising the home electric motor. I suppose people compared their motors—you know, "I have a three-quarter-horse-power motor," "I have a 1½-horsepower motor," "I have a three-brush motor," "I have a seven-brush motor." You put the electric motor at some central location in your house, and then you could buy attachments. This Sears Roebuck catalog shows a sewing attachment, a vacuum cleaner attachment, an egg beater attachment, a fan attachment, and so on. We don't do that anymore. We don't even see the electric motors in our homes. We go to the kitchen to grind the coffee beans to make a cup of coffee, or to make a cake. It turns out that an egg beater is really a pure electric motor with a simple attachment on it, and a coffee grinder is really a pure electric motor with a little grinding blade. But we don't think of them as motors. We think of them as the appliances that help us accomplish our task.

I look forward to the day when the computer is like the electric motor. We will no longer advertise the home computer or the office computer; rather, we will advertise, say, a better drawing package, or a better music package. Or we might have a checkbook, or we might have a daily calendar or address books. All of these devices will really be computers, and secretly they will all talk to one another and synchronize their activities. But they will look like fairly simple devices, though actually they will require even more powerful computers than we have today. I look forward to that time.

Toward a More User-Centered Technology

I was curious about how the transition from technology-driven designing to a more people-focused approach might occur. I was particularly interested in Norman's view of how insights and methods from psychology can be incorporated into the design process.

There is a very long and complex answer to that question, and the truth is that the complete answer is not known. It is often very difficult to get technology-centered people in industry to understand this field; we don't really have appropriate methods to address these issues, in any event. In fact, let me focus on the appropriate-methods problem.

You ask how methods, say from psychology, can help. I'm finding more and more that psychology isn't the most relevant discipline; rather, it is anthropology's observational methods that appear much more important—field observation. The real problem is trying to understand people in their everyday settings—at home, at the office, on the playground, in an automobile, or in a school setting. To understand how people operate in these everyday settings requires you to follow them around, watch them, and try to understand what tasks they're trying to accomplish and thereby to better understand what their real needs are. You can't do this in the laboratory because in the laboratory you can set up artificial situations and you pose only the questions you already know enough about to ask. But for designing information technology, the real problem is learning what the appropriate questions are in real-world situations. You cannot do this by questionnaire methods, either; you can't ask people what their needs are because on the whole they don't really know. If you ask a person, say, in office work what their frustrations are, what they most want, they might tell you they need some better tool for making a form or for making corrections in a form. Whereas if you actually look at the total situation, you might discover that the form itself is completely unneeded. So the answer to the question is complex, but it really does involve fieldwork and observational methods. We need observers who follow people, or groups of people, for periods of time, becoming acquainted with their work habits, making notes, making audio-tape recordings, and where possible making videotape recordings. The observers then try to understand what is really going on and how new technological developments might be of assistance.

Now, anthropologists and psychologists and scientists in general have different research agendas than the practitioner who wishes to introduce new technology. So the anthropological researcher's studies assume there is going to be a complete and accurate transcription of all the records that have been taken. This is an unbelievably tedious process—it can take tens of hours of time to transcribe one hour of videotape. I think this is really inappropriate when we're simply trying to understand the tasks and trying to know what we should introduce. Second, anthropologists (and social scientists in general) don't like to change what they're observing. They feel their role is simply to observe what goes on and to report on it.

But as a technologist my whole goal is to introduce new technology and thereby change the situation. And the only way I can find out whether my change is on the whole beneficial is to make small experiments and introduce changes and see what the results are. So the point is that I believe the methods are well known but the actual techniques are not really well developed. When asked if there are any research methods or techniques that can help designers foresee how technology will be used, Norman responded:

I don't know of any technique to predict the novel uses people make of technology. We can use the observational techniques I mentioned earlier to understand the *intended* use of a technology, but in fact every successful technology is used in ways completely unanticipated by its inventors. The telephone was thought to be a broadcasting medium; it was thought to be so important that every town would have to have one. It was anticipated that people would gather in the town square every evening to listen to the news. In my book *Things That Make Us Smart*, I look at what happened to the new technologies of the past century in the decades following their introduction. From this review I have concluded that it is impractical to try to predict the impact of any new technology. The best we can do is try to be flexible so that people can indeed use new technologies in unexpected ways. For the designer, this means you shouldn't even try to guess; what you *should* do is hope that your technology will be so successful that people use it in ways you never thought of—and then be alert to that. So what happens is that after the technology is introduced, we watch it to discover if it's being used in some clever way we hadn't thought of. Then we can try to make it better on the basis of our new understanding of its use. So we should think of this as a wonderful challenge and opportunity—*design never ends*. Even the most successful design will continually have to keep evolving continually in response to new practices.

Comparing the utility of his present work with Apple to his previous academic research, Norman noted:

> I find the area of design to be exciting and challenging and important. I was motivated in part by a desire to apply the academic research I had done. As soon as I started to apply it, I found how deficient that research was, how impractical many of the ideas were, and how many holes and gaps there were. The main point about academic research, I discovered, is not that it's wrong—it isn't; it's often very, very accurate and reasonable. The main point is that it leaves out so much that's essential to applications. Academic research focuses on tiny little pockets of knowledge. But when you actually wish to design something, you can't afford that luxury, just concentrating on only one little aspect and ignoring the rest. Your product has to work in every situation, and it has to fit into the space allowed, and it has to be manufactured at a reasonable cost, and it has to work in harmony with all the rest of the design and with other devices. This confronts the researcher with an exciting challenge: to face up to the complexities of real life.

Natural, Effortless Design

As so much of his work has addressed the ways in which design does or does not work, it seemed especially appropriate to ask Norman for his view of what constitutes good and bad design.

> Design actually has many components, so it isn't so simple. To begin with, let me not underestimate the importance of aesthetics in design. But with aesthetics it's more difficult to define what is good and bad, it is so tied to cultural norms and cultural values. One era's good design may be another era's bad one. So aesthetic judgments are to some extent relative. I find, though, that aesthetics is absolutely essential, that a design pleasing to look at and pleasing to hold seems easier to use. If you have to fumble with it, if you have to ask, "What do I do now?" or if you have to remember something, that's a sign of poor design. In fact, the easiest way to find examples of bad design is to look about your environment and find where people put up little signs and notices. Posted signs are an indicator of bad design.
>
> The measure of good design is simply how easy it is to use a product. It's also how visible the product is. This actually is a paradox because the very best design from the point of view of usability is the one that goes unnoticed. It appears so natural you never think about it, you never stop and notice the device that gave you so much pleasure. So unfortunately, the designer will be rewarded by the fact that people completely ignore the presence and impact of his or her work. But that's truly the sign of a good design—so natural, so effortless that you hardly notice the design.

John Seely Brown: User-Centering Design

John Seely Brown has spent much of his career exploring and applying advanced concepts, particularly those from artificial intelligence (AI), in industry and education. He earned a Ph.D. in Computer and Communication Sciences from the University of Michigan in 1972, and after periods as an assistant professor at the University of California, Irvine, and as a Senior Scientist at Bolt Beranek and Newman, he joined the staff of Xerox's innovative Palo Alto Research Center (PARC) in 1978.

Brown is now Director of PARC as well as Corporate Vice President and Chief Scientist at Xerox Corporation. In addition to his work in industry, Brown cofounded, and from 1986 to 1990 was Associate Director of, the Institute for Research on Learning, a nonprofit institute affiliated with Stanford University and the University of California, Berkeley, that conducts research into the principles behind lifelong learning.

Brown has authored and coauthored numerous books and journal articles addressing the relationship of learning, technology, and design, and he has served on the editorial boards of a number of journals, including *Artificial Intelligence, Human-Computer Interaction,* and the *Journal of Educational Computing Research.* He is a Fellow of the American Association for Artificial Intelligence and is also a member of several boards of directors, a diverse array of advisory boards, and a range of professional societies. Owing to this unique set of qualifications, Brown has on a number of occasions been called upon to give congressional testimony on the impact of information technology on education and science.

Portrait of John Seely Brown.

(Photograph by Brian Tramontana, courtesy Xerox Palo Alto Research Center)

Xerox PARC, Ubiquitous Computing "Tab."

(Photograph by Brian Tramontana, courtesy Xerox Palo Alto Research Center)

I began by asking Brown about the activities of Xerox PARC.

> The Palo Alto Research Center has five laboratories, ranging in their interests from atoms to culture. So it's a fundamentally cross-disciplinary effort that spans everything from theoretical physics to sociologists, anthropologists, and even an applied historian now. If I had to say there is one thing we do, it is to really understand how to enhance our ability to create value in the office.

One of the most intriguing concepts to emerge from Xerox PARC in recent years has been the notion of *ubiquitous computing,* a program to "dematerialize" computers, getting them out of boxes and embedding them unobtrusively in work environments to support people's work practices. Xerox PARC's prototype system comprises three elements of different sizes: tabs, pads, and boards. The purpose of each of these is set out in Xerox's literature.

> Tabs, which are about the size of Post-it™ notes, are designed to function like scrap paper. Notebook-sized pads and blackboard-sized boards are designed to enhance collaboration. For example, the LiveBoard™, a computational blackboard, can be used by people in meetings to facilitate the exchange of information, ideas and documents.[6]

Commenting on this concept, Brown said:

> From a ubiquitous-computing point of view, I would say what we're after there is part of rethinking and reexamining how value gets created in the office. It's an increasing appreciation of the fact that technology is finally getting powerful enough to get the hell out of the way. And so what we're looking at is how to blend work practices with technology so that the technology disappears—becomes transparent, if you wish. The technology is there to enhance our ability to be creative, to connect with other people, to learn from each other, and to learn from our own selves, à la Donald Schön's sense of "the reflective practitioner," now extended to the reflective group.
>
> So we're looking more at the kinds of work practices that will underpin the knowledge economy and how to amplify those. This requires, I think, going beyond the individual to really understand how we engage diversity in the workforce. How do we engage multiple points of view? How do we use each other's insights and triangulate our cognitive spheres to make maximal sense of the world at this moment in time? And so the technology is meant to fade into the background both literally and figuratively.

Communities of Practice

Whereas many participatory design processes focus on the individual, much of PARC's work seems to address groups. I asked Brown about this, and he replied:

> Well, it's not so much the group we address as it is what we think of as the "community of practice." I'll have to describe it through a two-by-two matrix,

where on one axis you have explicit and tacit knowledge and on the other you have individuals and the group, let's call it, or the team. What you find is that we in technology—and even design, to a large extent—have become preoccupied with at least two if not three of those quadrants. That is, we think a lot about the explicit-individual relationship—explicit knowledge for the individual; many of our tools are aimed at that. We think a little bit about the explicit knowledge for the group, which has to do with business-process reengineering, the collection and dissemination of "war stories," the total quality movement, and the dissemination of best practices. And then there is a little bit of honor given to the tacit knowledge for the individual—this is the third quadrant. But the quadrant that has been completely missing is the role of the tacit across the group. And much of our real knowledge is distributed among a set of players who come together around shared tasks and artifacts to get work done. It's almost as though knowledge lives in the social mind, in the artifacts around us, as though knowledge really emerges in practice through action (by *in practice* I mean in action around shared tasks).

We've overlooked that whole quadrant, tacit knowledge for the group. The force of this omission really begins to take hold when you think about how informal work, where I think most of the value actually gets created, is really done. It's the conversations we have around the coffee pot, the conversations we have in the hallways, the serendipitous meetings in the hallways, and so on. Curiously, if you step back and look at an office or a modern-day workplace, you'll find we don't spend that much time in our offices. In fact, we don't spend that much time alone. And yet virtually all the tools, even the collaborative tools, are still focused on the individual. And those that do exist explicitly for the group focus more on explicit knowledge—E-mail, cc notes, all this kind of stuff—and they don't try to enhance the emergence of knowing in action, where we participate with each other in the environment.

I've been struck for the last few years by a wonderful quote by Paul Allaire, our chairman and CEO, that says, "Workers know more than managers know that they know." Now, that's not asserting the workers have more knowledge; it's asserting that workers *know* more than managers know that they know. That can also be flipped on the other way: managers know more than workers know that they know too. But it's the notion of *knowing,* and knowing emerges in action.

Just because somebody doesn't have an articulate theory of something doesn't mean they don't know it. For most of us trained in the Cartesian view, if we don't have articulated intellectual knowledge, we don't really know because of the total separation of mind and body and the total worshiping of abstract knowledge over concrete knowledge or concrete experience. This Cartesian duality, which has so dominated our thinking in AI, in technology, and in fact in design is what we're really trying to blur. We're trying to destroy it, to blur the fact that knowing is in the body as much as in the head.

It's in the world, it's in our interactions with the world. In fact, knowing is a binary relationship. Knowing doesn't exist just in the mind; knowing emerges through activity. This is a key philosophical point that drives a huge amount of my intuitions and actually starts to do some justice to the whole notion of affordances in design. What is it that starts to emerge when I interact with a tool?

So our starting point is rethinking how the human mind works, how the social mind works, and how value is really being created. Then we put these three things together to rethink the causal forces in the environment that would enable us to enhance the right forces, to really enhance our ability to create value.

The Importance of Participation

Much writing about the work of the Palo Alto Research Center alludes to the concept of *situated learning,* and I asked if this was a central idea in PARC's work.

Well, what's central is that participation is critical. And participation happens in a context, so it's very much like what you discuss in your own first book about the move from modernity to postmodernism: How do you honor the context? How does the context shape perception? How does interacting with and in the context actually cause things to emerge that you didn't even know you knew? So it's much more a sense of shifting our focus from decontextualized, disembodied knowledge, which focuses on the individual's mind qua isolated mind, to full-blooded activity in a context. So much of our cognitive science, so much of our epistemology, our theories of knowledge and our theories of knowing have been driven by, "I think, therefore I am" versus, perhaps, "We participate, therefore we are." And so a fundamental kind of push for our design work as well is to honor the notion of action, situated activity, situated action, and to honor the emergent properties that can happen in correctly designed *contexts.*

One of the transitions that I see taking place in this regard is a shift from user-centered to user-*centering* design. This concerns how you design the context and the artifacts in the context so that it centers your interpretation of what to do. It's trying to extend the notion of affordances so that a building is well designed if it's centering for the user. It has nothing to do with user-centered design; that sort of misses. The key point is: How do you design a context? The same way a good artist does; by spending a lot of time on the periphery of a painting to make sure the eye is centered or guided to the crucial parts within the painting or drawing. So centering involves a sense of how the artifact pulls you into understanding it, or pulls you into using the right entrances for the right purposes.

Connected, Grounded Research

Advanced, theoretical research seems to be a critical aspect of PARC's work. I asked Brown about the nature and importance of the relationship between pure and applied research.

Well, that's a long topic. Let me just start out with a simple statement: I have no confidence in there being a principal distinction between basic and applied research. That may be one of the bogus notions we've been living with for decades, like Cartesian dualism, another piece of baggage we've inherited from hundreds of years. This distinction between basic and applied research is, to my mind, brain-damaged. One of my colleagues, Arno Penzias at the Bell Labs, once retorted, "There's only two kinds of research: that which gets applied and that which doesn't. So what's this 'basic' bit?"

It's hard to describe without diagrams, but I tend to think of research along three dimensions. The first dimension is incremental research versus radical or reframing research. With reframing research, you're willing to totally reframe the problem, to challenge background assumptions, to think out of the box, and to find something that is completely different than what you started out doing. With incremental research, you stay totally within the extant paradigm, you accept the status quo, and you make minor steps within that framework.

The second dimension is the difference between grounded and what you might call *open-loop* research, where you do research driven by the desires of your own community. Most basic research in the United States today is driven by problems that the community finds interesting. It has become a very inward-looking, relatively detached, open-loop program. The opposite end of that spectrum is grounded research, and by *grounded* I mean grounded in real phenomena, so that you honor and engage the world in the problems you're investigating. Said differently, innovation lies as much in the world as it does in the head.

If you look at physics at the turn of the century, much of the great work was done with physicists working on real problems and then having the freedom, if not the responsibility, to follow the problem. And when the problem led you to suggest reframing radically some fundamental hypotheses about how the world works, you did it. Now what we're looking for is what we call *pioneering research,* which is radical and grounded. When research is grounded, you find that multiple disciplines can often come together and focus on that, and the grounding in the world itself pulls people's views together.

If you're just doing open-loop research, then you almost never get good synergy across the disciplines. But if you triangulate on the world from multiple disciplines and if you honor the world and realize that invention lies as much in it as in the head—going back to our earlier comments—then practically magical things can happen. Now, we do not think of this grounded research as the same as *mission-oriented* research, in which the mission is the ultimate Holy Grail. With grounded research, the world is the ultimate Holy Grail. The key here is to understand the world still but to let the world do more of the work for you. You're letting the world guide you, you're letting the world coordinate you. In some senses this sounds overly philosophical, but if you look at the history of research in the United States, or around the world, it's really quite amazing how research has become more and more detached from real phenomena. Here again, a research philosophy merges with our appreciation of the context, the power of honoring the context, the power of listening to the world and working with diversity, with different points of view, on real problems.

If one has that point of view, many of these questions that you have in mind don't compute any longer. Basic-versus-applied doesn't compute anymore. The question is: How much are you honoring the world? How much are you willing to "marinate" in real problems, then step out of those problems and think radical thoughts when need be? And then, how much are you willing to reconnect to make sure that your ideas have an impact? That's the trajectory we're looking for, and in that trajectory you can have radical ideas and a very short-term payoff. So it's not a question of this being long-term or short-term research. Some of our most fundamental ideas can pay off in a year because we have reframed the problem. Once the problem is reframed, then *bang!*—some of those reframings can move with blinding speed to have an impact.

The Role of Learning

One of the key focuses of Brown's writing through the years has been the process of learning. I asked Brown why this area is so important to the design of new technology.

If you go back to one of my first comments, I talked about our focus on how value is created. If you step back, you'll recognize that we're living in a world where the accelerating pace of change is real so that, to use a cliché, about the only thing that's constant today is change itself. We find ourselves in a context where virtually all the skills, or at least most of the skills, we learned five years ago are at best questionable today. If this is true—and surely in the world of information technology it is—then the ability to learn faster than other organizations may be the one real sustaining competitive edge that an organization or corporation has. So the shift from asking, "How do you create products?" to "How do you learn faster than anybody else?" is the way you maintain your competitive edge.

It brings you back to the kind of interpretive stance that asks, "How do you interpret what the world is doing? Where are the trends? Why are those the trends? What are the causal forces at work? What do people really need? What are the latent needs?" And so on. That requires a keen ability to listen to the world and its backtalk. It means being able to leverage diversity, to interpret in the best possible way the significance of a certain set of actions in the world and then, from that set of experiences, to learn rapidly and to move to action.

So if you think about the Industrial Revolution, our competitive edges came from scale and mass production. Now the cliché is "mass customization"—that is, how do you serve market segments of one? I'd say that we maybe missed the boat there. But I think the higher-level point is: How do we learn with agility? How do we learn rapidly? How do we learn to reframe our understandings of the world and put those reframings into action? So I think the ability to build the learning and the unlearning organization is going to be the key to success in the twenty-first century.

Facilitating Conversations

I asked Brown how, in his view, the technology of the future will be different from that of the present. I was especially interested to learn about the transitions that will result from the realization of Xerox's *ubiquitous computing* concept.

Well, the technology will differ in several ways. One is that the technology is with you in the context. This is not just mobile computing we're talking about. We're talking about working in a kind of information environment where you have "scrap" computing surfaces everywhere providing windows on each other and on the past, much like Mark Weiser has written about.[7] Now, if you use the surface metaphor, what we're trying to do is facilitate conversations in the present in terms of how these surfaces all interact with each other, so I can scribble things and then have my scribblings connected to my secretary, Janice, up the hall and be able to pass notes back and forth. These same connected surfaces also enable me to reach back in the past, to review things instantaneously, to get the information I want at my fingertips. That is one class of activity that fits within our current frame of looking at the world. And there's nothing surprising there.

What may become more interesting is: What ways of reflecting upon past experiences enable you to learn more from them? So if you look at things like the types of informal meetings we have around the hallways, these are driven by our electronic whiteboards, which have the ability to pull up things that have happened in the past and replay parts of the conversations that were happening as we were scribbling on the whiteboards. Then we automatically know who was there, so part of the context is wrapped up with the actions, and we can use contextual information to retrieve things as well as content information. When you do this, you suddenly start to experience a new kind of active learning medium. I like to think that what I'm describing, and what we're striving for, is the creation of a new kind of work medium that really enhances our ability to become reflective practitioners, that helps us move from experiences to insights, to better interpret the world.

Knowledge is situated, and understanding is socially constructed; therefore learning is social. With this triad, the role of a conversation becomes critical. What I've found so startling is the realization that most of what you and I know today we have learned from each other, often in conversations. And, yes, admittedly many of those conversations are anchored in real-world experiences or books that we've read. But it's the conversations, it is engaging in a telling-listening activity that really starts to shape this understanding. So much of what we're trying to do is to honor the power of anchored, copious conversations, if you wish.

These aren't necessarily verbal conversations. They can be collections of written notes, they can be actions. I use *conversations* broadly, a little bit like Donald Schön talking about listening to the backtalk of a situation in design. When good designers go to design something, they can tell if it fits right. They can almost have a conversation with that design in the context and understand its fit and congruence, or the lack of fit. It's that sense of being able to have a conversation with and in the context, which good designers do all the time. Schön talks a fair amount about this, and I may be changing his words slightly, but the intuitions are the same. So this notion of a conversation with the world is a very metaphorical concept.

Asked to elaborate on this notion of conversations, and in particular how it guides Xerox PARC's interface design work, Brown said:

The essence of a conversation is to be able to sense a breakdown, interpret the breakdown, and move to take the breakdown as an opportunity to extend the conversation. A good conversationalist is often one who can make apparent what he or she has just misunderstood so the other person can read the misinterpretation or misunderstanding and know how to make the next move. This underlies, I think, the power of the conversation. This is not a question of natural language. Underlying conversation is a reciprocal ability to signal the status of reception, to cue the other not merely that it's their turn to speak but as to what has been understood and what hasn't been understood. When something hasn't been understood, how is that signaled? How do you know quickly that something has been misunderstood? And what kinds of clues are given as to why it has been misunderstood? With that, think back on a really good conversation and you'll see how this is actually played out.

Now curiously, we in user-interface design try to build these idiot-proof systems that never have a conversational breakdown, which is of course impossible. The systems make no effort to reveal when you're walking down a dialog path in an interface that has started building a set of suppositions that really diverge from where you want to be at that moment in time. So what we're looking at is ways to build more transparent technology that reveals more about its current state, technology that lets you participate with it and better interpret where it is. It's as simple as that.

Put another way, what we're trying to do continually is to design environments that support improvisations and that honor the little, local problem-solving leaps of faith each of us makes every time the rubber hits the road. That's what we mean by building these Glass Box user interface systems: when the "rubber hits the road" there's always going to be a little bit of friction, there's going to be a little bit of misalignment. And the catch is: How do you bring things back into alignment? Well, that requires revealing what the misalignment is really about.

Technological Sensibilities

I commented to Brown that he seems to focus much more on a discussion of learning and thought processes than on technology itself.

> What I'm talking about, which is the heart of Xerox PARC, is sensibilities. Technology is created around a set of sensibilities. That is what everybody misses. They think technology is driven by itself. And if that's the case, then that too is one class of sensibilities. What we're trying to do is to create a context with a different set of sensibilities, where the high priests of technology are let loose. So it's not that we're downplaying the power of technology. Quite the opposite—we've got world-class technologists. But the catch is: What are the sets of eyeglasses we use to make sense of what we need to do and what we have done? And the part that's never talked about is sensibilities. What I'm trying to give you is a little view of a set of sensibilities that are at radical odds with the sensibilities that you'll find in a lot of other research laboratories.

It struck me that this sensibility of Xerox PARC, with its focus on the context in which work is situated, is almost diametrically opposed to the technology-driven approach that seems to have been adopted by most companies.

> This will sound very abstract, but there's a sense that when you come to honor the context you let the world do more of the work for you. Good design has an amazing ability to transform constraints into resources. That's the best aspect of contextually sensitive postmodern design: the ability to stay with the context and let the context do some of the work for you. It's also a key part of what we're trying to do with ubiquitous computing. And with ubiquitous computing—there are many different takes on that concept, by the way—we're trying to find ways to let technology disappear by having it participate with us in social practice. So the transparency of technology is part and parcel with how much it is connected to our social practices. And that requires seeing how we use the world around us to get the job done.

A simple example—it will sound like a red herring—occurred when we went out to work with the people who troubleshoot our copiers; we call them *tech reps* at Xerox. When they're troubleshooting copiers or machines, it turns out they have to take lots of measurements. You would first think that a beautiful idea would be to use a laptop or notepad to have them scribble down the results of all their measurements so that they don't have to remember them. You could have them use a job performance aid to suggest what next to do and so on. But what we've discovered is that these tech reps are remembering the data by spinning stories, narratives, as they troubleshoot, stories that make sense out of the measurements taken thus far. So they create a story that basically weaves together explanations of the symptoms and of the measurements that they're making.

Now what happens here is that this story is part of the troubleshooting process. The story is beautifully matched to how the human mind remembers things. And in the end, the story happens to be an ideal artifact that can be disseminated amongst themselves afterwards. And so here's a clear case of what I've been talking about. I could have gone in as a highfalutin technologist and built a brilliant, artificially intelligent job-performance aid. In fact, I was first asked to build one. But before we went down that path, we asked, "What's really happening there that people who've looked before aren't apt to have even noticed?" And we saw the clever ways that these tech reps were using bricolage, things around them, to make their job easier, and some of these things were invisible even to them.

That's more the spirit. Now we're moving on ways to help people better communicate their stories. There's some very low technology involved—actually a two-way radio is used—that lets each member of a work group spread around a district be in each other's periphery. So now we have a tool that supports the social periphery of the workforce, where you can move from the periphery to the center when you have an insight about the struggle that this guy's having and that you happen to be able to overhear. It's a completely different approach than building an intelligent agent that steps in and does the job for you. So it's a different set of sensibilities, you're correct. But it's hard to drive a clean wedge between the two camps. It is a different set of sensibilities *and* it is a sense of honoring the context, just as designers do, considering ways to transform constraints into resources.

Beyond Technology Transfer

It is not uncommon for large corporations to ignore or set aside ideas generated by their research units. Xerox, in particular, has been singled out for not developing ideas such as the Xerox Star interface, which PARC created and which became the basis of the highly successful Apple Macintosh graphical user interface. I asked Brown about the extent to which PARC's ideas are now being adopted and developed by Xerox.

Let me say a couple of things about that. One is that this notion of the power of the conversation comes back to the whole notion of what technology transfer is about. To us, more and more, *technology transfer* may be an oxymoron. Maybe the real issue is: How do you set up a set of authentic dialogs between the research community, the development community, the strategy community, and the marketing community? When you do that and you have the chance to have a set of authentic conversations, then innovation happens through coevolution and coproduction. And so part of our philosophy leads to a different sense of what technology transfer is about.

Now, that's not really the question you asked. If you look at our heartland copier business, for example, most people think PARC has had very little to do with it. But that's not true. Our ability to take substantial market share back from the Japanese once they targeted us is extraordinarily unusual in the United States. That has happened in part because so many of our ideas of design, both inside and outside the machine, have taken hold in the corporation. In fact, our high-end Light Lens copiers have thirty microprocessors and three levels of Ethernetwork, all inside the box—plus a user interface that is unquestionably superior to anything you've seen on the Macintosh.

So these ideas are now penetrating the core of the company as well as its periphery. On the periphery of the company, for example, are our Paper-Works products. Our latest products there allow you to move seamlessly from images of documents to the content of documents—it involves incredibly sophisticated optical character-recognition stuff that understands the context and content of the document in order to facilitate its interpretation.

We're beginning to see a whole class of strategic alliances coming out that likewise are based on a set of fairly radical ideas developed over the last few years at PARC. So we're now seeing our ideas come out in all kinds of ways, not the least of which is having helped create the fundamental strategic intent of the corporation around the document—shifting the corporation from thinking of the technology for processing paper, to technology for processing documents, to the document itself as technology. That is probably the biggest shift that any major corporation I know of has ever undertaken, and PARC played a major role in that repositioning. In fact, you might say that in the past PARC was in the periphery of the corporation, but now we're becoming more of an integrating force for the corporation.

6 | Thinking Strategically

One of designers' laments is that they are compelled in their work to anticipate the future and embed that vision in form. Not surprisingly, designers often guess wrong. John Chris Jones addresses this point in his book *Design Methods,* noting:

> Often a design process ends with the thought "if we had known at the start what we know now we'd never have designed it like this." One of the main reasons for seeking new methods is to avoid this "learning too late."[1]

Though Jones wrote these words in 1980, the problem he describes is as prevalent as ever and, in many ways, it is becoming more pronounced as design becomes more complex and the rate of technological change accelerates.

To combat this problem, several methods have emerged in recent years that provide more strategic and anticipatory approaches to design. These include John Thackara's Cultural Engineering, based on the premise that design is primarily an exercise in managing knowledge; Larry Keeley's Strategic Design Planning, a process that explicitly explores the broader contexts within which design is situated; and Peter Schwartz's Scenario Planning, an approach that can be used to explore the likely changes that will occur over the lifetime of a design. This chapter features conversations with Thackara, Keeley, and Schwartz in which each discusses the nature and applicability of his approach.

John Thackara: Cultural Engineering

Though John Thackara has been a central figure in design theory for over a decade, his educational background is not in design but in philosophy and journalism. Thackara became involved in design while working as an editor at a publishing company that produced magazines and books on architecture and design. He later was editor of Britain's *Design* magazine before cofounding Design Analysis International, a London-based consulting firm. Thackara is now Director of the Netherlands Design Institute in Amsterdam, for which he has organized the highly regarded Doors of Perception annual conferences that the institute has hosted since 1993.

Thackara has lectured, broadcast, and written widely on design, technology, and culture. Among his many projects have been the influential books *New British Design* and *Design After Modernism,* both of which he edited. Thackara has served on the Advisory Board of London's Institute for Contemporary Arts and is a Fellow of the Royal Society of Arts. He has organized numerous exhibitions, including ones at the Centre Pompidou in Paris, the National Museum of Modern Art in Kyoto, the AXIS Gallery in Tokyo, and the Victoria and Albert Museum in London. Thackara has also been a consultant to numerous firms in the private sector, including IBM, Japan Airlines, Canon, NEC, Rover, and Alfred Dunhill.

Portrait of John Thackara.
(Courtesy Netherlands Design Institute)

Asked how he became involved in doing design work himself, Thackara said:

> Basically, the traditional job of the journalist, and in particular of the editor, is to observe the world in question, the domain, in a relatively neutral way and perhaps to commission people to comment about it. And that is not an interventionist point of view. But both when publishing books and when editing *Design* magazine, analysis of the activities of designers and their clients and of their interaction with their environment threw up the fact that there were problems: the state of awareness of the profession; the awareness of clients; and the capacity of the environment to allow the design process to operate well. There were unresolved difficulties. Publishing books about the field and then publishing a magazine about it, I became increasingly frustrated at simply reporting the problems of the process rather than doing anything about it.

Design Analysis International

> Over a period of about six or seven years as a critic and journalist, I came to the conclusion that there were things I could do as an interventionist to fix it up. Design Analysis International (DAI) was born out of this experience.

Along with a colleague and friend in Japan, Tadanori Nagasawa, and an original partner in the U.S., Steven Holt, we decided that a service could be provided for the exchange of information and for the production of exhibitions, seminars, and conferences at the interface between design and its external environment. The five-year life of DAI involved a mixture, about fifty-fifty, between consultancy and production. (*Production* means creating events in which we are the partner or the sole proprietor. *Consultancy* means giving people advice.)

One of the key concepts that underpinned the founding of DAI was Thackara's realization that the business of design is more concerned with information than with products. Asked to comment on this, Thackara said:

It is quite easy and appropriate to describe a design as a process that ends up with an object. But designers and companies and consumers have a continuously evolving series of relationships with the material world. We never have just one car. Nothing is ever fixed in terms of improving the relationship between design and industry. One is talking about a process rather than a fixed event. The design process is the sum of the relationships between designers and technologists and communication people and marketing people and consumers. When I say that design is an exercise in managing knowledge, it's because a designer does not invent atoms or create fundamental concepts; a designer orchestrates material and immaterial things that already exist. He or she gets materials together, uses different media to communicate about a product, and marshals physical and information input so that out of the other end comes products or services.

Central to DAI's work initially was the notion of *design brokerage,* which Thackara created. Addressing the origin of this concept, he said:

Ten years ago, when I looked at the dysfunctional aspects of the design process, in which clients had unrealistic or impossible expectations and designers did not understand the motivation and expectations of their clients, a brokering role between the two seemed a good idea. Later I actually became less convinced of that. Practice, experience, and observation persuaded me that the fewer intermediaries there are between designers and their clients the better. Brokerage sounds like a good service, but in reality it more often confuses the matter than simplifies it.

Thackara refined design brokerage into the concept of *cultural engineering.*

The experience with design brokerage informed the theory and practice of cultural engineering, which involves the creation of an environment in which designers, clients, and third parties such as scientists can interact more effectively. Creating a chain in which I as intermediary stand between the designer and the client doesn't really add value. But to have somebody who creates, who really helps to make their relationship work better, that is what cultural engineering is about; it's about creating a better one-to-one relationship between parties.

Exhibition Design and Management Consultancy

As noted, there were two main areas of activity for DAI: exhibition design and management consultancy. I asked Thackara if there was any particular significance to the choice of these areas. He replied:

> In response to a gap in the market, we decided to produce exhibitions in much the same way as a film producer produces a film. We produced exhibitions about design, architecture, media, and so on because there was a demand among venues and sponsors for temporary exhibitions. People did not have the particular expertise in their organizations to coordinate the researchers, the curator, the set designers, the graphic and computer designers, and all the others who are involved.
>
> I think exhibitions are a research activity in their own right, even when they are exhibitions of existing objects but certainly when they are idea-based, which most of our exhibitions tried to be. The process of developing a story and then developing the hard and soft bits of an exhibition to tell the story is a complicated and exciting process with parallels to the way that people develop shops or offices or other environments. The concept, words, pictures, moving images, objects, space, and of course people—putting all those together in an exhibition was complex but fun. Certainly, the reason why we liked working with architects to create an exhibition was that they had an understanding of space and movement and behavior that is not generally so well understood by traditional exhibition designers, who are often graphics-based—"books on walls" and all that.
>
> The parallel consultancy activity grew because in working with these museums—often owned either by cities or, in some cases in Japan, by private companies—it became apparent that owners were failing to program these institutions strategically. Nine times out of ten, museums and galleries are real estate propositions or civic architectural monuments. So much effort and money goes into getting the structure erected and maintained that very little is thought about the purpose and organization of its content. Financially, this could be disastrous: a big gallery can go through as much money in running costs over five years as was needed to build in the first place. But nobody thought properly about this. Producing events for these places, we realized that they had no real idea why they were doing one exhibition rather than another. Or, more crucially, what was the purpose of their activities in a more general sense—for the local economy, for education, for culture in their vicinity.

Discussing these questions with clients, we developed alliances with other consultants to do with writing the program for a museum or an institution to go with its building. One gives lectures to people about the absolute necessity to decide on the program before you decide on the building, but that's the ideal scenario; more often what happens is that they build the building and then wonder what to put in it. Very often one does a study for a city—for example, what a design museum or an architecture center would be about—and then they do or don't take it forward. To us this was mortifying at first, until we came to realize that the wastage rate of concept studies for new buildings was incredibly high. If you have a chance to realize it, it's usually because someone's built a building already and can't decide what to put in it.

We did a number of projects in Japan, for example, not only for city governments but also for larger corporations. These clients came to the realization that while they wanted to develop a profile as knowledgeable or culturally sophisticated companies, they did not have the expertise to develop a program, let alone to structure individual projects. Our clients were sufficiently sophisticated to know that they did not just want to give money to people and have no further involvement. So we were the party that created the relationship between our clients, such as a big company and either an individual designer or a group of designers or an institution, which had a life through time. Our job was to ensure that the expectations of the research and activity agenda were well understood between all parties at the beginning. If somebody is going to have a relationship over five years with an art school or with a museum, it's important to make sure that people's expectations match up at the beginning, because if they don't you can be quite certain that they'll quickly run into trouble.

I was interested in how DAI actually did its work, as it did not have designers on its staff or drawing boards in its offices. I asked Thackara if he could give me an example of their work process.

Yes, I can give you a good example. A Japanese lighting company called Daiko came to us saying that they wanted to modernize their catalog so that it would appeal to architects. Because we were not graphic designers, we were able to say that it did not make a great deal of sense to change a catalog if the products in it remained the same. We advised that you can, on a step-by-step basis, integrate the design of your products, the design of your literature, the design of your other communications, so that the whole becomes a more coherent aggregation of activities, but that it doesn't make a great deal of sense to do one without the other. This was not a revolutionary insight on our part, and this sort of exercise is not terribly complicated; it basically means helping the company manage its suppliers, whether they be designers or technology suppliers, in a more balanced way to achieve more coherent objective. That's all I really mean by design management and

In Harmony: Light, Technology, Design
1990 Professional Lighting Fixtures Catalogue
DAIKO

cultural engineering. We did not stand between the company and its designers, but we made sure that they both understood what the other was trying to achieve. Very often, once that understanding develops, one can withdraw from the situation.

Though DAI did not itself employ designers, one of the distinguishing characteristics of their exhibition work was the involvement of teams of leading designers. Commenting on this, Thackara said:

> It's my selfish desire to work with good people, and it's my experience that good people will respond to an interesting challenge even when money, or even prestige, is in short supply. One of the myths about "stars," be they designers or architects, is that they spend their entire life doing glamorous and creative work. The reality for most people, including me, is that behind every glamorous project something mundane goes on to pay the rent. It's not frankly that difficult to persuade people to take part if it's a good project, if everybody concerned will learn from the experience, and if they'll be working with interesting people. Frankly, I don't think we ever made any serious money out of exhibition production, and I don't think any of our associates did either. There is a payoff shared between interest and money. In our work, at least, if something is incredibly well paid, it's rather unlikely to be incredibly creative. Show me a rich designer and I'll show you hidden projects for soap powder or nuclear power promos.

Design Strategy

While Managing Director at DAI, Thackara was also appointed Director of Research at London's Royal College of Art. Describing this work, he said:

> We did some work as consultants for the Royal College of Art, a postgraduate school that specializes in art, design, and communications, about their research strategy; we looked at their problems creating an environment in

(above left)
View of *Leading Edge* exhibition organized by DAI at the AXIS Gallery, Tokyo, Japan.
(Courtesy John Thackara)

(above)
Page from Daiko's lighting catalog after DAI's intervention.
(Courtesy John Thackara)

which postgraduate art, design, and communications students could work in research programs collaboratively with companies from the outside. The difficulty was that there was no expertise either in the writing of the research agenda or in the management of projects once they were created within the school. There is a proven need in many types of industry, and for that matter in other organizations like city governments, for the expertise and ideas that the design and communications students have. It's just that nobody can quite figure out how to bring everybody together in a mutually beneficial way.

Following our initial investigation, I began as a Consultant Director of Research to develop a policy and an infrastructure which would support these multidisciplinary, collaborative programs. We then recommended to the school that actually what was needed was something slightly more well resourced than just an office with myself in it. We came up with the idea of a Design Strategy Centre, a management entity that would support and promote the extension of these research programs on an international basis. And this was very well received as a concept, but sadly the funding that it required fell victim to the recession in the UK, so the project was never realized. But many of the ideas in it to do with organizational forms—the collaborative, multiparty programs—did take root, and in fact several examples of that model now exist at the RCA. One is Design Age, a multiparty consortium on design for older people which has made a tremendous impact under its Director, Roger Coleman.

The Netherlands Design Institute

In 1992 Thackara took up a position as head of the newly formed Netherlands Design Institute, based in Amsterdam. Explaining the origin of this institution, he said:

> The Dutch government had over a period of five or six years determined that there was a gap in the national infrastructure. It wanted to promote design as an important cultural and economic asset of the country. After rather protracted discussion, the government came up with this institute, voted the funding (about 1.5 million dollars per year), and made a deal with the city of Amsterdam, which provided the building. Five years elapsed from when the idea was first raised.

I was interested to learn what the Dutch government's aims were in initiating and funding the institute.

> It's intended to benefit Dutch design, recognizing that Dutch design is indivisible from the European design market. Our original brief was rather "soft" because our primary funder is the Ministry of Culture. But culture and economics are not easily divided, and so nobody can predict precisely how the

benefits will accrue on a national, or a European, or a global basis. We have to create criteria for evaluating our activities so that we can measure our success at various levels. Our primary role is to benefit Dutch design, culturally and economically, but we will only achieve that end through acting internationally.

When I came on the scene, it was to inherit a broad constituency of government and professional support, a consensus that an institute was a good idea but not a precise agenda for its activities. I was fortunate to be able to draw on my experience consulting externally for a lot of these types of organizations, city and national governments in Europe and Japan. Those experiences persuaded me that what the Dutch needed was not just a traditional promotional body that simply exhorts people to value design, publishes traditional magazines, or organizes design exhibitions like everybody else. I was appointed director with the understanding that we would create a different type of value-adding, based on research activities that would create new knowledge about the design process as it affects the cultural economy. We have been funded as an organizational entity since the beginning of 1993, and we became an operational institute in the summer of 1994 when our building, a former art museum, opened on the Keizersgracht canal in Amsterdam.

We have a small central staff of eight people who support several research clubs, or action groups. At any one time, there may be twenty or thirty people active in the building and more involved in projects externally. We're an organizational center, a kind of command-and-control organization through which we help to make programs happen with other institutions around the world and with other companies. Our aim is to have established within a few years a small organization which while small maintains quite high-level programs on an international basis.

The Netherlands Design Institute has already made an impact on the design debate through its Doors of Perception conferences. The first of the annual events was held in 1993, and a CD-ROM based on the conference was awarded a Design Distinction in the Interactive Media category by *ID* magazine.

One of the strengths of Thackara's approach is that it sidesteps the discipline-based approach to design in favor of a more collaborative, multidisciplinary approach. Commenting on this, he said:

> One of the very strong elements in this institute is our unwillingness to acknowledge so-called design disciplines as the basis of our work. We are organizing ourselves instead around thematic issues such as communication, the applied arts economy, or the communication environment. We don't say, "This is something that graphic designers deal with, and this is something that product designers deal with." We look at design markets such as business communication or product innovation or ecodesign—domains of cultural and business life in which many disciplines necessarily work together—and define

our role as finding ways in which they can work together more creatively and more productively. It's absolutely crucial to do that.

I feel rather strongly that it's not realistic to expect a good architect to be a good marketing person; nor is it sensible or desirable that a marketing manager should aspire to be creative, like a good graphic designer. You need to create a situation in which both can both play to their strengths. People are going to be specialists. You cannot turn the clock back and make everybody a Renaissance generalist. The modern world is so technically complicated that people will have specialized knowledge. The point is that they cannot be effective in isolation. The activity of enabling them or training them to work together is very important, but it doesn't replace the need for deep individual skills.

In this institute, for example, I have a constituency of people like jewelry designers and ceramicists, who think about objects on the body, or pots, or whatever; and then I have a big agenda to do with interactivity, computers, and communications. And people say to me, "How can you possibly have these two programs in the same institute?" And I reply, "We will be ahead of everybody, because the two can work together and learn from each other."

Back to the Object

I was interested in Thackara's view of how the rapid expansion of electronic media will affect design, particularly as this has been an underlying theme of the Doors of Perception conferences that he has organized.

I edited an anthology called *Design after Modernism,* which had a subtitle that disappeared in the publishing process, *Beyond the Object.* But I've come to the conclusion that I should now be writing a book called *Back to the Object.* I now recognize that there is a difference between acknowledging and even celebrating that we live in a media-saturated world and failing to nurture and protect the body-bound element of human identity. Of course, we have to understand that media systems and artifacts are filling our world, and designers have to intervene. But that is not to say that this process is self-evidently a good thing for human beings, or that machine intelligence is superior to body-bound intelligence.

One thing that designers, and in particular applied artists, understand is physicality and sensual aspects of objects. And insofar as media saturation is a problem for our culture, if we can create objects—albeit very smart objects—and environments which are very physical and which, so to speak, root us to the ground as human beings with bodies, then that's probably a good thing to do. I've been reading about this notion of "hard" and "soft" artificial intelligence. In the '80s, when I was thinking about design "beyond the object," people were speculating that technology could create artificial entities that did everything that human beings do.

Maybe it's because I'm getting older, or maybe it's because science is becoming more modest, but the balance seems to be swinging toward a soft AI that complements rather than replaces what we can do ourselves. Even if it were theoretically possible to simulate human intelligence in a machine, to do so is a waste of time because technology used as a prosthesis to a body-bound human intelligence has far more potential. In terms of cost-effectiveness, to spend years of effort and countless money recreating something, namely, the human brain, that already exists is absurd. Why do it? What's the point? Why not accept that we live in bodies and have an amazing intelligence and capacity for thought in that respect? Why don't we just create extensions to that existing intelligence? Hence, "back to the object." The body and the real and the material world are where our priorities should lie. We should put virtuality into the here-and-now, not the other way round.

The Future of Design

As a longtime observer of emerging trends in design, I asked Thackara for his views on the future of the design professions.

There is a generalized crisis for design and architecture, whose professional structures do not correspond to the tasks at hand. So the potential future for design is to be a central player in the innovation systems of the industrialized world, to be a kind of guiding light in the remodernization of cities. But I think there is a real danger that design, particularly as a profession, with that name, could be marginalized if it does not modernize and redesign itself. A profound and long-term process of reeducation and professional development is required if design is to exploit the opportunities that exist. I am optimistic but also have doubts about whether we will succeed in modernizing what is a rather conservative environment. I come back to what I said before: we don't want all designers to turn themselves into cyberneticians; we want them to be designers who do a special thing very well. Perhaps the task of exploiting that skill in a dramatically changing world falls slightly outside the traditional design world onto design managers or business in general.

Furthermore, one needs to distinguish between design as an activity and designers themselves. It causes terrible arguments and trouble when you make this point, but you *can* have a design process without designers. The problem is not the value or importance of the designer's input to a building or to a product. Design is vital to their quality. No, the problem is the inability of designers to operate in these environments or to explain and justify their input. Look at the building industry, where this is happening more and more. "Design-and-build" construction companies are dominating the development of complex and expensive buildings, whose clients are increasingly reluctant to get architects involved. Of course, an architect has conceptual skills that a design-and-build general contractor lacks; an architect has a vision and understanding of human needs, which the general contractor also lacks. But architects are becoming marginalized by the complexity of the environment, in which they have seemed incapable of acting in a group context or in a team. Their input is thus reduced to a low level. That's why there is a very real consciousness of crisis in the architecture profession. They know they are being squeezed out of the system. You can make a similar argument about product designers in manufacturing or graphic designers in communications: their skills can be codified into computers or copied by people who aren't trained as designers.

I don't, on the other hand, know that it's so much more serious for designers than it is for scientists. The ability of a scientist to affect the development of a drug or a compound is limited, too. The world of technoscience is so complicated that no individual controls it. The overproduction of knowledge is also a crisis for capitalism itself: extracting profit from a system in which innovation proceeds ever faster is a real question. It's not obvious to me that the interactions between investments and innovation can be sustained at present levels for very much longer. There's no profit in it when things change too quickly.

Design/Philosophy

To conclude, I was curious to learn how Thackara felt his background in philosophy had benefited his work in design.

I would like to be able to say that philosophy makes you an "ideas person," but candidly I don't think anything about my philosophy training specifically helped me. It probably made me unemployable for all other aspects of life except what I now do. Insofar as philosophy inclines one to look for broader pictures or broader patterns, then it's a useful sensibility, rather than skill, if I can put it like that. This is very important within a professional environment like design, where people tend to be specialists cut off from each other, and there is strong environmental pressure for people to operate in an isolated way. A philosopher is disinclined just to look at so segmented a picture of the world, and he has the training to look for the pattern that lies behind things. In particular, the concept of design as process is something that a philosopher isn't going to be frightened by.

To somebody with a basic philosophical training, it is not a surprise that the world is such a complicated place. But it would be self-evidently untrue for me to say that I understand things better than people who studied design. I just see things differently. Philosophy led me to expect things to be abstract and confusing, and therefore I'm not worried about it. Whereas a designer with a conventional education is taught to try and impose order on things which are perhaps not orderable.

Larry Keeley: Strategic Design Planning

Larry Keeley is President of the Chicago-based Doblin Group, a firm that practices Strategic Design Planning. This process, which Keeley and his team have evolved over seventeen years, helps Doblin Group's clients to understand the changing nature of their environments and, using this understanding, to transform their industries through strategic applications of design knowledge. Among the firm's clients have been Xerox, Amoco, Motorola, Hallmark, McDonald's, the National Park Foundation, and Texas Instruments.

In addition to his work with clients, Keeley is a frequent lecturer on design, a board member of the American Center for Design, and a past board member for the Design Management Institute. He is also a member of the Board of Overseers for the Institute of Design at Illinois Institute of Technology (IIT), where he serves as an Adjunct Professor, teaching graduate courses in design strategy. IIT is the only institution in the United States to offer a doctoral degree in design and the only program in the world to offer a degree in design planning, and Keeley and the staff at Doblin Group are closely involved with the Institute of Design both as teachers and advisors.

I began by asking Keeley if he could describe the type of work Doblin Group engages in, which he did by analogy to more traditional design approaches.

Portrait of Larry Keeley.
(Photograph by Daniel Chichester, courtesy Doblin Group)

If you ask a design firm to reinvent something like an airline without special methods, they'll come back with superficial answers. They'll tell you about the zippy new colors of paint they can put on the planes, the cool new livery they can put on the crew people, and about the terrific new ticket jacket they've designed, and why all this, if accompanied by a great and eye-wateringly expensive new advertising program, might be seen as something new and different.

To us at Doblin Group, that's vastly different than something that can reconceive the *concept* of the airline. For example, the ways that it intersects with rail travel or bus travel, rental cars or personal autos; the way that it intersects with hotels; support for healthy, pleasant meals or meetings; and the role of information systems for advanced reservations. We would focus on improved approaches to "tailoring," so that people get what they want to eat, the kind of things that they want to read, the ability to have an office while they're traveling, to have incoming and outgoing phones and faxes, and to have different kinds of very comfortable seating and improved kinds of personal storage. With a comprehensive rethink of the industry, these kinds of personal preferences would be routinely delivered to travelers. Clearly, if you want to solve a complicated system like this, then you need deeper, stronger, and more thorough methods.

Some of the methods we use help us to understand the structure of people's everyday lives, to learn the things that people actually do. Not what they say they do but in fact what they actually do. Methods like video ethnography are very important to us. Often we use fairly commonplace technologies in surprising ways. Sometimes we send microcassette tape recorders by Federal Express, along with disposable cameras, to people whom we want to have document something in the world. So we send them a disposable camera and a digital tape recorder, we have them walk around and take twenty-four shots of something or other, remarking upon the shots as they're taking them. They then send it all back by Federal Express. It's one of the ways we came to understand the relevant issues at America's National Parks in a hurry and at relatively low cost. You can get thousands of data points back within a week or two this way, all of it observational, so it is qualitatively different than mall-intercept studies, focus groups, or other forms of research that designers (quite properly) loathe.

One time we studied all of the third grade and all of the fifth grade at two of Chicago's private schools by sending disposable cameras home with the students and having them photograph the places where they do homework. In one week we had two thousand data points that our social scientists could then analyze—all done with no muss, no fuss, and at little expense. So there are new kinds of technologies around for doing ethnographic research. The methods themselves go all the way back to Margaret Mead and other anthropologists, but the tools have changed and so the methods need to be updated.

Some of the methods we use have been invented here at Doblin Group, others we have borrowed from our colleagues at the Institute of Design at Illinois Institute of Technology, where Charles L. Owen has been the methodologist in residence for twenty-four years now. He has produced things like structured planning methodologies that still use, believe it or not, mainframe computers. Those approaches have the horsepower to help us unpack a very complicated system. So we can analyze a gasoline station, a retail firm, a restaurant chain, and so on to determine which ideas or subsystems within an overall new construct can be improved *together* and which in fact are in conflict with one another.

People are often critical of Doblin Group and its methodical nature without understanding it. Those who do not understand Doblin Group will make the mistake of thinking that we're so scientific, so methodical that we subordinate design challenges to computers in a deterministic or mechanistic way. Nothing could be further from the truth. What we're trying to do with our methods is deal with complexity in a way that allows us to solve a complex problem while addressing it in the richness and fullness of that complexity. The truth is, *no* designer or engineer, in my judgment, can reinvent something unless and until it's broken down to the point where their common sense, logic, intuition, spirit, and brilliance can wrap around it adequately. In the end all things come down to feeding a problem to somebody in a way that allows them to transform it, to twist it, to do something surprising with it. Our methods allow us to begin "unpacking" enormous complexity and breaking it down to those little parts and pieces that we can assign properly to people who *do* brilliantly transform them. Some of the magic comes in the ways we can pull scores or even hundreds of such innovations together, allowing us truly to transform an entire industry.

Doblin Group believes designers have the vision and values needed to invent holistic, integrated concepts for the future, fixing many parts of everyday life. Part of our mission is to give them the tools and the methods they need to be coequal with financiers, marketers, organizational design experts, researchers of diverse types, engineers, and manufacturing experts. We see a time coming when designers will be accorded a similar level of professionalism and entrusted with huge systems-reinvention responsibilities.

Design Briefs

The focus of much of Doblin Group's work in recent years has been on the development of design briefs for their clients. Asked to describe the nature and purpose of this work, Keeley said:

> Briefs are nearly religious artifacts here at Doblin Group. They are inevitably the focal point for everything we learn, think, do, and believe about a case. There are many different kinds of briefs, each of which has a different purpose or degree of impact. We make a distinction between what we call an *emerging industry brief,* an *activity brief,* and a *product brief.*
>
> An emerging industry brief is a very broad survey of how entire industries will collide and evolve and change. We do these for some of our largest clients that want to have Doblin Group scanning the world for them to help them to know where they should invest to create or participate in emerging multibillion-dollar industries.
>
> An activity brief looks at some part of people's day-to-day activities, to explain how everyday things that they engage in are changing. So we can look at retailing, education, money and banking, home and family, travel and leisure, or at various other activity arenas and talk about how they are being transformed. For clients, this is the gift that keeps on giving. If you study an area of activity, it can be used very effectively for creating breakthrough product genres—inventing things that haven't happened before. There is a huge difference, for instance, between the study of changes in home entertainment and the study of VCR operability. By studying entertainment generally, you make breakthroughs; by studying VCRs, you only make improved VCRs.
>
> Product briefs are ways to understand the basic shape of an industry and the players within it, but the focus is on products per se, along with the services, distribution channels, and personalities associated with them. This

type of brief tries to identify what's coming next within a category or a field, all directed at helping our clients change the ground rules for their competitors. Many of our clients want to have product briefs. But our smartest, most aggressive clients prefer activity briefs or emerging industry briefs; these provide much broader opportunities, which typically are associated with larger-scale disruptions and much larger returns on investment.

What is a brief, really? A brief, to us, answers some simple questions: what's desirable to users? what's next technologically? and if it were our company and our money, what would we do with scarce resources? The brief tries to get the concept right, not the details. The company then knows how to bring in the right kind of internal staffers, internal talent, project managers, and external resources to act on what has been identified and, in fact, go beyond the brief. The brief never gives explicit answers, but it very carefully outlines the nature of some key goals, the kinds of things needed to make these come to life, and the ways that those things interrelate. So the people who are running a railroad, for example, can understand the teams they should have, the tasks that those teams should engage in, and the kinds of goals that they should be held accountable for. That turns out to be really helpful to the average person running an enterprise.

National Park Service Design Brief

To clarify their use, I asked Keeley if he could cite a case in which Doblin Group has generated a design brief.

I can talk about work that we've done in this regard for some of our public, pro bono cases. Doblin Group, along with Institute of Design graduate students, helped develop strategies for the National Park Service and the National Park Foundation, for example. These strategies provide *radically* different ways to run the entire system of America's National Parks, ways that still honor the cherished values that guide the Park Service. Instead of, as is now the case, ending up with a thirty-million-dollar annual shortfall, they could conceivably generate annual surplus funds running into the tens of millions of dollars. This is a pretty radical transformation.

The National Parks are going broke, and we had to rethink them fairly fundamentally. As I say, every year they are thirty to forty million dollars short in terms of operating budgets, and we wanted to give them an alternative that would keep them from being utterly dependent on the largesse of Congress, an elusive quality in recent times. So we talked about what is wrong with the parks, and we talked about contrasts between what they do and what other enterprises do. We urged them, for instance, to learn from Disney's strategy, which is to take a primary product like *The Lion King,* and create hundreds of artifacts derived from it. This is now done by Disney annually, with a new primary product (*The Little Mermaid, Beauty and the Beast, Aladdin,* and so on) brought to market each year.

Meanwhile, the National Park Service requires you to go to the National Parks and talk in person to a ranger—a rewarding but very costly approach to teaching. They have a whole range of stories and can take any one of them, like the current popularity of dinosaurs, and extend them across hundreds of artifacts and dozens of distribution channels. That would allow them to reverse the financial patterns, to switch from being totally deficit driven— they're increasingly unable to do fundamental things to keep our National Parks from deteriorating—to being very positive in terms of cash flow. Even though we're recommending things that would cost them a great deal more to operate, they would make so much more money that ultimately it would be a fundamental transformation.

This would be very difficult to pull off, because it requires some big changes within the Interior Department. We have to change much of what they do, all their operations and systems and so forth, in ways that they have no resources to address. So the plan demands that we generate those resources. We wrote a second plan for this and provided it to the National Park Foundation, an enterprise run by CEOs of various large-scale companies. We had to help these leaders think about things their companies could do and what partner companies they could involve to make some break-throughs come along, such as fundamental new technologies for rangers. This approach makes the parks innovations we've proposed more practical and achievable.

In addition, about a third of the things that would absolutely need to be done are illegal because some laws governing the parks date back to 1916. So a final challenge was to address the legal changes that would be needed to give the parks innovations a reasonable chance to work. Altogether, it took a four-volume set of design briefs to help our National Parks conceive a shift from financial dependency to strong, positive self-sufficiency.

In terms of scale and scope, this parks project is typical of the type of transformation that we try to map for our clients. Often it blows people's minds that design-type people could deal with complexities of this order. Who would have thought that *designers* could get really amazing break-throughs involving such big shifts? For us, the goal is to break down such complex "multisystems," make them accessible, reinvent them, and make the innovations exciting. When you do it right, it's fun for clients, and it starts to actually work.

The Origins of Strategic Design Planning

I was interested to learn from Keeley how Doblin Group came to develop the Strategic Design Planning approach.

First, we were very fortunate to have been founded by Jay Doblin. Few people seem to realize that Jay Doblin was the leading design methodologist in this country. Fewer people still seem to understand the extraordinary personal history that Jay Doblin had. Arguably, there have been three great design firms in the history of the world (a uniquely American history). Unarguably, the leading design firm at the birth of design was Raymond Loewy and Associates, certainly the most influential firm of its time, the '40s and '50s. In the '60s a new firm emerged called Lippincott and Margulies that invented the field of corporate identity. Then in the '70s the leading firm, with offices in seven countries, was Unimark International. And amazingly enough, Jay Doblin was a founder or the creative head of all three of those firms, and he's the only single individual who connects them. Of course, while he was at Unimark he was also Director of the Institute of Design at Illinois Institute of Technology, which he transformed from the sort of quasi-Bauhausian art school Moholy-Nagy built to the leading design-methods school in the world, which it remains today.

Doblin Group is the fourth business Jay Doblin founded in his design career. Since his death in 1989, both Doblin Group and the school he directed have prospered and grown a lot. They're pretty unrecognizable since Jay's death. Both have become larger, more visible, and more influential. Yet each in its own way owes an enormous intellectual debt to Jay, who saw that the design field was fast becoming superficial and irrelevant. His insight, which occurred in about 1979, was that designers are trained as generalists but to survive had fragmented themselves into specialists. Firms could no longer survive just by being a general design emporium, the way Raymond Loewy's did. In Loewy's day, whether you wanted the plates in your corporate cafeteria designed, the shrubs in the front yard, the uniforms, the graphics, or the products, you could go to a single source. It was "one-stop shopping" for all your design needs.

That has ceased to be possible in modern times. And yet designers are still trained, typically, as generalists. Commercially, in order to survive, they're split into specialized firms, covering, say, corporate annual reports, packaging, information design, form design, product semantics, product form, product value engineering, and on and on. Jay's insight was that clients need an integrated, powerful, innovative approach to design, yet the only way to achieve that reliably demands a small blizzard of focused firms. This puts an enormous burden on the client to know who's out there and to get them together into a "lean, mean fighting machine." Of course, that almost never happens.

It's one thing to have an insight; it's another thing to know how to put it into practice. We were very fortunate that Xerox, in effect, put us into business in 1979 when the firm consisted of Jay Doblin, me, and a part-time secretary. Xerox asked us to think about all of their design processes and the way they should use design. The trigger issue for them was that they had spent a half a *billion* dollars to develop a new copier line, worked on for five years by twelve hundred engineers and others, then it got all the way up to the chairman. The CEO at that time, David Kearns, looked it over and said, "Jeez, I think it's ugly." And the chief of design, then Arnold Wasserman, said, "Oh no, sir, it's quite lovely." Whereupon David Kearns replied, "Well, I think it's ugly." So there ensued a clarion call to try to figure out who could come forth and say whether or not this thing was ugly. They brought in Jay Doblin, who was to endure a full day of indoctrination and then give his verdict. At the climactic moment Doblin said, "Well, it's fierce ugly, but that's hardly the point. The real issue is: how could you guys possibly have spent five years and half a billion dollars with twelve hundred people making a copier that's so hard to operate?" To the credit of a number of the senior people at Xerox, they understood that they had a deep and pervasive problem in their design processes.

So our work with Xerox really invented this weird field that we now have practiced substantially the same way ever since. And the way it works is simply to begin by understanding the industry, a simple thing to say but very hard to do. In particular we try to understand how design is used in the client organization—to understand users and their needs, to understand, in effect, the difference between what's being done and what might be done.

The Strategic Design Planning Process

I asked Keeley to explain the Strategic Design Planning process that he and his team have evolved. He described in detail the four typical phases they go through.

Phase 1: Plans and Briefs

The figure on the following page presents the four phases of our process. In the first phase, clients come to us. They're confused about something, and they want a plan to address it. Actually, they usually want to address some basic trigger issue, which often must be expanded a bit. For us, all effective plans have their basis in a deep and profound understanding of user needs, so we use a cloud shape around the term *user needs* in the diagram to indicate that there are proprietary Doblin Group methods involved in this stage. They are typically done by our social science team, which features people from a range of different disciplines.

After we do a plan, which will take four to six months and cost anywhere from three-quarters of a million to a million and a half bucks, we will produce briefs. The plan itself is an integrated, powerful sense of what we think ought to be done within an industry. But unfortunately, there is no single place you can go to pull it off, and the client cannot do it by themselves normally. On those rare occasions when the client can do it in-house, it will still

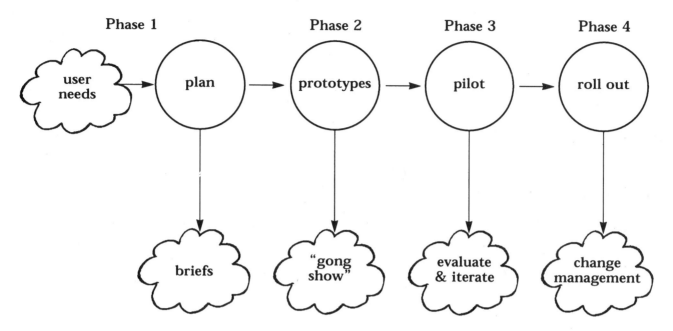

Phase 1 **Phase 2** **Phase 3** **Phase 4**

user needs → plan → prototypes → pilot → roll out

plan → briefs

prototypes → "gong show"

pilot → evaluate & iterate

roll out → change management

**Doblin Group's
Strategic Design Planning
process diagram.**

(Courtesy Doblin Group)

have functional departments that have to participate in special ways. So we "atomize" the integrated, powerful plan into special resources that do exist, either the firm's own resources or outside specialists we help identify. Thus, briefs are used to inspire a large, multipart team to invent the individual innovations needed in a case.

We then use the briefs to solicit bids. Typically, we're soliciting those bids from famous design firms—product design firms, graphics design firms, interface firms, multimedia development firms, architectural firms, interior design firms—whatever a case calls for. Bidders are only shown the portion of the case that relates to their speciality. This is one means of security control: you don't want to reveal the entirety of the case to everybody who's bidding. So the portion that relates to graphic design is given to graphics design firms, for example.

So we'll give the brief to four or five graphic design firms, and they give us back proposals. We gather all the bids for the design briefs, and some happy day you select the winners, and they're all brought together, and we use special methods and special team building exercises to forge them into a group. Now you have a product designer, maybe, and an architectural designer, and a graphic designer, an interface designer, an information systems designer and God only knows what other kinds of specialists all sitting at the table. Then you share all the briefs with that team. Now everybody is included in the entirety of the case.

At last we have our reinvention team, and the exciting part of the work begins. One of the mysterious and magical parts of design planning comes because these teams know that in Doblin Group they're working with a design-savvy organization. They also know that they don't have to do the front-end business analysis, which if they're honest about it they'll admit that they're not brilliant at. So we've taken away their most cumbersome, expensive, and difficult stage, and we've also taken away the burden to make fancy comps. With us they know they can work both rough and loose—they can send us electronic files, work in progress, they can give us tissues, they can give us roughs. We can go to their place, or they can come to our place, and everybody knows they can have casual meetings—all of which is a way of lowering the cost structure of the design firms we're doing business with. We do not lower their fee structure, however, so in general they get very profitable work with us.

At this point the true teamwork begins. As it does, specialties no longer matter so much. We don't really care if the architects are thinking of graphic design ideas, or the product designers are thinking of interface ideas. We think such boundaries are artificial, and we don't pay too much attention to them once the team is formed. We only pay attention to them as we compose the team. Now we can go to work building breakthroughs.

Phase 2: Prototypes and Gong Shows

The next stage is very expensive, but it is the most exciting part of our work. The goal is to create a series of *prototypes* that tell an important new strategy story. Designers have one truly remarkable skill that they themselves often do not fully appreciate the sophistication of—it is the power to *simulate,* to take something that does not exist and to make it utterly, totally understandable, believable, and concrete so that those with less imagination can understand it. The power of a prototype is that it takes a strategic idea, then makes it real, instead of abstract.

If you take a look closely at what strategic planning firms like McKinsey, Bain, Boston Consulting Group or Booz Allen provide—for usually about two million bucks—it's typically some abstract models and some spreadsheets. It is a known fact that only about 5 percent of the American populace is truly comfortable with mathematics. Let us assume that the distribution of math-comfortable folks in business is three times what it is in the general populace, which is I think a very generous assumption to make. That still means that only 15 percent of the people in business are comfortable with arithmetic. Yet almost always what people provide as a result of supposedly strategic analysis is econometric modeling.

We think that is completely unhelpful to people who don't understand what's possible. Worse than that, we think it's the wrong way to get the future to show up. The times we live in are characterized by extraordinary and rapid change. Our life and times are changing faster, in the opinion of many observers, than any prior time in the history of the world—much faster even than in the Industrial Revolution. The issue today is not to fix the *economics* but to fundamentally reconceive the products and service *concepts* themselves.

As a result, most firms, including Doblin Group itself, have a wrong strategy today, or at least an *incomplete* strategy. This is not because they're stupid, not because they don't mean well or work hard, but because of the near infinity of amazing things now possible and achievable. As an aid to this open-ended strategy challenge, we published our Strategic Palette Model years ago, covering areas like materials, manufacturing, features and functions, channels of distribution, and so on, that help companies imagine doing more in a rigorous fashion. Most companies, however, think they deserve a giant medal if they put in a Total Quality Management program or if they've got a business process reengineering exercise going on. Of course, most of these efforts are *valuable*, but they usually do not truly reinvent a field.

Prototypes are a way of showing what's possible and of doing it in a way that is grounded in user needs. With any prototype you ought to be able to take a before and compare it to an after to show that the after is self-evidently superior. Any individual prototype should get people nodding, to say, "Wow, how cool" or "Oh, is it possible to do that?" or "Jeez, the customers would love that" or "Wow, this would be something we could do with the factories we already own." Prototypes always help people get excited about individual innovations. But many firms use prototypes. We now go beyond them to create a big simulation we call a Gong Show.

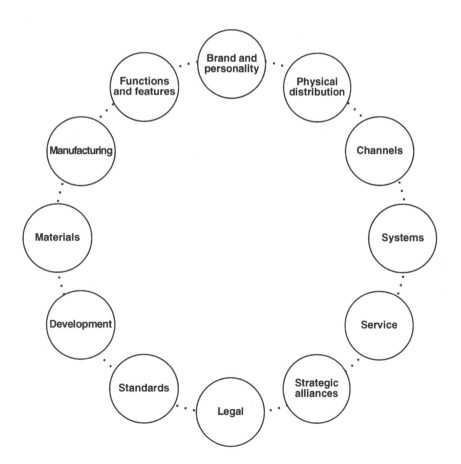

Doblin Group's Strategic Palette Model.

(Courtesy Doblin Group)

In a Gong Show, we typically gang together between sixty and 150 proto-types, although normally around eighty to a hundred. Gong Shows have two purposes. One is to present individual examples of a new strategy. The other—the magic part of a Gong Show—is to present all the prototypes together, collectively, to illustrate a powerful new strategy, a way of separating the client organization from any other firm in their industry.

In our very first case for Xerox, the Gong Show consisted of about 140 prototypes done by seven different design firms and by as many as four hundred of Xerox's own internal designers and engineers. In 1981 we took top management into one of their own conference rooms (they have conference rooms there that are ideally scaled for running hang gliding contests) and gave them a presentation on one side, reminding them of the strategy that we felt was pertinent to their industry. We then opened the electronic conference room walls and walked them into a full scale trade show with two full product lines simulated, plus graphics and changes in brochures, in research models, and in virtually every kind of artifact that might be part of the future of the company—advertising, packaging, supplies, catalogs, accessories, all simulated so that anyone could see how the company could all come together.

It was a fascinating experience and the culmination of quite an amazing process. And to this day that's still what we do, and it's what makes Strategic Design Planning different from strategic planning. We don't show spread-sheets, and we don't show abstract models. We show real stuff that is founded on a profound understanding of user needs and that uses every kind of design needed to make it come to life.

This is one way that we give everybody in the client organization a shared mental model of both what is possible and what's desirable. This helps forge a unity of purpose and sense of commitment about taking specific action. After you get people to agree to do something that everybody understands, then comes the hard work of turning that into structures, strategies, skills, and systems of reference that will make it happen without the use of millions of dollars worth of outside consultants. We do all of this using some propri-etary methods, typically invented here at Doblin Group, occasionally invented at the Institute of Design, or at places like Palo Alto Research Cen-ter. These methods give the client organization some solid insights about what the users need, how those needs are changing, and so forth. We try to leave this knowledge behind in the company. Creating a complete organiza-tional change process comes later, after we've gotten people to agree that they're interested in the future we've simulated.

In this phase we try to make sure that the client organization, all on its own, without the reliance on millions of dollars worth of outside consul-tants, can routinely create ideas *better than the prototypes*. This usually demands that we transfer the design processes and research methods into the organization, along with a deep and pervasive conviction about the strategy and the intent of the company and make sure it all takes root.

This approach to Gong Shows, while fantastic, has often proven overwhelming. People love them, but at the same time some are occasionally daunted by the scale and scope of changes being called for. So sometimes now we scale those back a little bit, do lots of little shows or do them in different ways. As a firm we have turned the rheostat up on the creation of really great prototyping strategies. These are a very essential part of helping people envision different aspects of the future. Increasingly, we're looking at approaches to visualization that involve special effects or simulation modeling or rapid prototyping of many different types. I think everybody in design these days understands the role of rapid prototyping, but I doubt that very many people understand the idea of prototypes as they apply to *strategy simulation*, as opposed to their more common application to products or messages.

When you simulate future strategies, you allow clients to climb inside an imaginary future state and see how they might serve customers, how they might delight and surprise them, all while going far beyond the customer's own ability to imagine experiences they might have.

Phase 3: Pilots, Evaluation, and Iteration

In phase 3 we create and evaluate pilot tests of innovations. What we're trying to do with the chief executive officer now is to come up with some meaningful subset of all we've shown, something that can be done coherently and deeply to launch a big change in the world. So when we think of the word *pilot*, we're thinking about maybe twenty individual items that serve as a valid test of the new strategy in the world somewhere. To do this we throw a tight fence around an aspect of a customer's experience, then change all the things that matter inside that fence. This pilot phase can typically take a year. Often it involves small-run manufacturing, plus the launch ads, changes in distribution channels, pricing adjustments, support for the sales people, some special alliances if needed, and so forth.

Once the pilot test is unveiled, we have a chance to evaluate the results and iterate again. Here the same methods that helped us to understand user needs in the first place can be brought back. This helps us understand whether or not customers are responding. Often they may be baffled by some details, delighted by something, or left with their needs still not really met. So in the evaluation process, we're looking at measures that we think are meaningful, the kind of measures that too often designers don't want to spend time understanding, let alone measuring. For us it's stuff like customer satisfaction ratings, market share, margin, and so on. These are measures that chief executive officers care about a lot, and so do we. Ultimately, by being willing to take such business measures seriously, we help elevate the design field to a level where it is taken more seriously.

Phase 4: Rollout and Change Management

The final stage in the process is *rollout*. This usually features a national or international launch of some substantially altered (evaluated and iterated) item or series of items. Then comes the weirdest stage of all, which we term *change management*. This is itself an entire subfield of management consulting, with dozens of specialized practitioners. The truth is, it is a bit mind-boggling that in order to do decent design work in this world, you have to know a lot about work structures, incentive systems, measures, skills, staffs, management styles, and other organizational dimensions far removed from anything taught in design schools. But the miserable fact of the matter is that you've got to know this stuff to have true impact. So we may spend up to a year transforming the client's organization to ensure that they have the right internal measures, the right incentive systems, the right structures, the right skills, the right staff, and the right folks to make sure that these innovations with proven market relevance don't end up like skin grafts that simply don't take.

This is done in much the same ways that a McKinsey or other management consultants would work, but we've had to adapt those methods to our own approach. Here again, all of those bottom bubbles in the Strategic Design Planning process diagram are associated with proprietary Doblin Group methods, and this one's no exception. But we do borrow from an amazing plethora of things out there in the world, such as team-building skills, trust exercises, time management exercises, team management exercises, decision environments, gaming and simulation, networks, computer-supported collaborative work—all kinds of interesting fields converge on that little bubble.

Back when Jay Doblin was still alive, we acted as if the *prototypes* were key. Our expectation was that the client would see the brilliance of the ideas and the systemic implications, whereupon, amid tears of gratitude, they would rush to remove all organizational obstacles to the immediate adoption of these important breakthroughs. Nice as this notion might be, the world doesn't work that way. The better mousetrap theory never was true and should never, ever be expected to work. The prototypes and pilots help people get excited—the true triumph, however, comes in the redesign of the enterprise. This has been a long, slow, important lesson for us to learn.

We use this simplified four-phase model to describe our process for people who have never heard of Strategic Design Planning. In reality, these phases overlap a lot, without clear boundaries or smooth handoffs. It's basically a little foggier than what we've drawn for you. But all of those things should happen and do happen. They just may not happen with quite the linearity that that model implies.

Design/Business

I commented to Keeley that his present approach seems much more rooted in the world of business than in that of design, to which he replied:

> Yes, but let me just emphasize one thing. I love boutique design firms and boutique designers. To me it's very exciting that the Michael Vanderbyls, the Lisa Krohns, the Tibor Kalmans, Rick Valicentis, and the others whom I think of as the individual luminaries of design are out there. That's a joy. The world is characterized by lots of different possible paths in life. Let me be real clear: if I were a designer and had that kind of talent, I would pursue a personal design vision in a hot second. I think it's delightful. However, it is seldom at the core of a great design plan. Our job here is to reinvent, reconceive, entire industries or product categories. It *is* more like business than design, yet you absolutely cannot do it *without designers.*
>
> One of the things that I just love about designers is that, whether they know it or not and whether they admit it or not, they're always designing for themselves. They're always designing stuff that they themselves would like to steal or like to keep. That's true of the environments they create and of the artifacts that they create—whether products or messages. Designers by and large are considerably less motivated by money than people even in other supposedly creative fields like advertising. I think that is an incredibly important, healthy, and necessary impulse. We have to figure out how to channel it a little bit. We also have to figure out how to watch out for designers failing entirely to take into account the customers' value system. But basically, I think the spirit, the heart, the soul, the pervasive sense of trying to make the world a better place that is characteristic of designers, is really an important force and is certainly central to our processes.
>
> Even if I were not successful in this field—and we've been lucky to be pretty successful—I'd stay in it just because I think designers are so cool. I think that they have figured out how to have balance in a world that doesn't have a lot of balance. Designers are socially responsible, in the main, and quite concerned about the life cycles of the artifacts that they create. I think that's healthy. Give our culture another thousand years and maybe everybody will be like that. But in the meantime, designers are a little ahead of the pack.
>
> Having said that, I do get aggravated occasionally by designers who presume that a particular style is appropriate to a particular situation and who assert that it is a valid approach in its entirety. Most designers are not strategic in their thinking about what kind of design matters in which situations. Worse, they don't know how to determine this. I'm not critical of designers per se; I'm just saying that for certain kinds of problems, the economic value of design as a field depends on our being able to defend our ideas. It's simple: when clients hire me I expect to be held accountable for the fees they pay me or the subcontractors on the team. This means I've really got to know what

matters. I can't guess. I can't wing it. This takes some doing, but it makes design important, and it helps designers get paid what they are truly worth.

Design Research

Research into user needs is central to the work of Doblin Group, and I asked Keeley to elaborate on their approach to it.

> We don't think it's sensible to design anything unless you've got a sense of what users need and want. We also think that marketing, the industry that purports to best illuminate what users need and want, is deeply, profoundly, and utterly flawed. This whole province of market understanding has historically been accorded to marketing organizations—marketing theorists in business schools and practitioners in marketing research firms—as well as to their number-one client, the advertising industry. I am incensed at the weaknesses, intellectual and methodological, in the foundation of what constitutes research in this domain. Most designers truly hate research for reasons that they cannot put their fingers on. And this hatred, this distrust, is in fact profound and well founded. Designers are quite right to dislike researchers and research as it is conventionally done because it violates the spirit of the enterprise of design. Research and researchers make a whole bunch of errors, probably beyond the scope of this conversation, that deserve to be roundly criticized.

> Here at Doblin Group, we believe that the problem, which is systemic and pervasive, will never be remedied until design asserts its own kind of research, research that is particularly thought about in the context of a design process and the questions and needs of thoughtful designers interested in those insights. So we've split the design process per se into lots of basic stages; then we've tried to invent new kinds of research for each of those. If there's anything that will clearly endure beyond Doblin Group, if we screw up somehow and we're gone, what I'm certain will remain is our focus on research methods, because we truly have created some new ones that are starting to revolutionize the way design is thought about.

The Organization of Doblin Group

In order to carry out the broad range of work that Doblin Group undertakes, Keeley has assembled an extremely diverse, multidisciplinary staff. Commenting on this, he said:

> One of the weirdest things about this place is that we've got about thirty employees, with a large number of different specialties represented. Any

student of organizational theory would tell you this is wacky. It's considered terribly unstable, and it's very, very difficult to know how to run it. Law firms are filled with lawyers, of course; accounting firms with accountants; strategic planning firms are filled with MBAs; research firms are filled with researchers; and advertising firms are filled with advertising folks, a combination of marketing folks and creatives. But we're filled with all kinds of weirdos, and for us a big part of the challenge is to have ways for the individual members of the team to even communicate with one another. How do you get a computer programmer working comfortably with a cultural anthropologist, an interface designer, a product designer, an architect, a journalist, a strategic planner, a demographic expert, and perhaps a sculptor? A huge part of what Doblin Group has had to think through is things like facilities and teams plus tools that forge a truly collaborative group out of this ragtag collection of diverse individuals. It's kind of fun because I always feel like I'm really lucky to be able to work with these colleagues of mine, all of whom know some field much more profoundly and deeply than I ever will. I think everybody else is similarly charged by their sense that they're in a special place and that they're surrounded by special individuals from whom they can learn a lot.

I asked Keeley how, with such a group, projects are organized.

It's very fluid. It changes all the time, and people are even brought in from a different case for an afternoon of help sometimes, or to offer a tiny piece of guidance and criticism. Doblin Group is extremely flat in terms of total hierarchy. Everybody in the place will be a team leader on something or other at some point. We actually have a number of levels in the structure we had to invent for our human resources programs internally. But there are no titles on anybody's business cards, and as you walk around the place, you see in an instant that there's no hierarchy. Nobody gets a special office or anything else.

There is a level of *responsibility* within cases that is assigned according to an individual's experience and expertise. There are people who can handle entire client engagements, and they're called "directors" for purposes of our internal human resources program. Separately, there are specialists within the firm who do something unusual like videotape analysis or systems design or product prototyping or something else. We like to think that the specialists here could make a reasonable living and could stay in that specialty all their lives. That's a very sharp contrast to strategic planning firms, where everyone is presumed to be seeking partnership and everyone is annually expected to move up or out, *up* implying more and more client engagement responsibility. We do not have that as a value system or an expectation. So we've tried to set up at least two major tracks. One allows you to be a better and better specialist, the other allows you to be a better and better generalist.

The Impact of Strategic Design Planning

Asked to summarize the impact of Doblin Group's work with Strategic Design Planning on client firms, Keeley responded:

> The convenient sound-bite answer is that we do two things. Number one, we try to think about a very comprehensive and systematic idea of what is possible and desirable. Number two, we pull together all of the many kinds of specialists that are necessary to make it come to life. How did we get there? We were lucky. Clients asked us to help them solve big problems and they sat still while we invented ways to do it. Xerox is an amazing firm. They've always been way ahead of others. They haven't been able to capitalize on it very well, but they understood Jay Doblin was a very special person, and they put us in business. Within the last six months, I had a visitor from Xerox. I walked him around what is now quite an enormous place with a lot of interesting laboratories and interesting environments. I said to him, "You created this. What do you think?" And he was astonished. They had no idea that they had invented this field and that it was so successful. You know, there are four or five firms around the world that are specifically saying that they're emulating Doblin Group in design planning, and we think that's great. This field will be much bigger a decade from now.
>
> Strategic Design Planning is a very practical, forward-looking way to invent new stuff at a time when the world needs to invent, reinvent, and reconceive everything. That's what I love. Everywhere I look, everything in the world needs to be reinvented because we can do it better now in some way or other. You can do it differently. You can do it digitally instead of electromechanically. You can do it with fewer resources, in ways that are more convenient for people and that are more responsive to their personal preferences, as opposed to following some marketing person's abstract mathematical representation of what people say they want.

Transforming Industries and Consumer Experiences

Given the broad scope of his work, I was interested to learn Keeley's definition of good design.

> To me, good design always transforms. It always viscerally affects users, makes them delighted, changes their activities, changes what's possible for them. Good design is always about changing user experiences positively. I define *users* very broadly, too, by the way, not just to denote those who initially use an artifact but also the rest of us who are victimized when it's chucked out.
>
> I also think good design is characterized by the way it permits client organizations to benefit financially. It ought to help firms to gain share, gain

margin, gain loyal customers, and I'm unabashed in my belief that that is a valid thing for designers to help them do. I will only associate myself with design that transforms industries and transforms customer experiences.

Peter Schwartz: Scenario Planning

Peter Schwartz is a futurist and business strategist who cofounded and is President of the Global Business Network (GBN), a consultancy based in Emeryville, California. The focus of GBN's work is corporate scenario planning and research into the future of the business environment. GBN is unique in that its project teams are composed of an array of strategists, business executives, scientists, and artists from around the world, with an emphasis on those who represent "divergent thinking."

Portrait of Peter Schwartz.

(Courtesy Global Business Network)

Prior to founding GBN, Schwartz was in charge of scenario planning for the Royal Dutch/Shell Group of companies in London, for which he conducted analyses of the global business and political environment. Earlier still he directed the Strategic Environment Center at SRI International, which, in addition to doing strategic planning for corporate and government clients, carried out research on consumer values, lifestyles, and the business context.

Schwartz articulated his view of scenario planning in the book *The Art of The Long View,* which was selected as the number-one business book of 1992 by *Business Week.* Though developed in the business and institutional context, Schwartz's approach has direct applicability to design, in particular to novel tasks and to those contexts where frequent change is expected. GBN cofounder Stewart Brand, for example, set out his use of the scenario approach in application to architecture in his book *How Buildings Learn.* Brand and GBN now offer seminars on scenario planning for design professionals.

I began my interview with Schwartz by asking him to define *scenario* and to explain why he believes the approach is valuable.

Well, we actually have a standard definition of scenarios which is: scenarios are tools for perceiving alternative future environments in which one's decisions might be played out. One of the keywords in that definition is *perceiving.* What we're really dealing with is what we *believe* about the future; decisions are always made on the basis of perception, not fact. We organize the world into a picture, and it may or may not be based on fact, but we act on the basis of that picture. If that picture's reasonably perceptive there's a chance we'll make a good decision and if not it's just gambling.

Second, we're dealing with *alternative future environments,* and the fundamental purpose of that is to recognize uncertainty. Most other tools assume that in some way or another that if you get the model right you can actually predict the future. Scenario planning assumes that that is *not* true, that you can't predict the future and that we live in a time of fundamental uncertainty. It probably always was so, but it was a matter of degree. Now it is relatively extreme, and so one needs tools that actually take into account that reality rather than denying it to assure that one makes better decisions. The last key word is *decisions*. The definition of a scenario relates to an actual choice one has to make rather than an abstract exploration of the future. The reason for scenarios and why we do them is that we really do live in a time of huge uncertainties. If we look back at the last couple of decades, the kind of shocks and changes and surprises that have really transformed the world are rather profound. I think that very few of us would deny that the future is going to be filled with at least as many of those surprises and changes. If one has failed to think about them one is likely to have relatively high regrets later on.

Developing Alternative Views of the Future

One of the key features of Schwartz's approach is the development of multiple scenarios, each of which presents an alternative future. He does this rather than trying, as most futurists do, to predict the single view of the future that will come to pass. Schwartz explained the rationale behind this by comparing it with another frequently used technique.

> One of the other tools that is often used is called *sensitivity analysis*. Let's just take a hypothetical example. Suppose the demand for a product is going to grow by 40 percent, and then you say, "Well, suppose it's 20 percent larger or 20 percent lower." So you're saying it might grow by 60 percent or it might grow by 20 percent. That's a range; that's not what we mean by scenarios. That's simply sensitivity analysis. That's taking one model of change and varying one measure of it slightly.
>
> You will find, in fact, that when surveyed (and there have been several academic surveys of businesses) a very large number of companies will say that they do scenarios. One report I saw said that something like ninety out of the top one hundred companies did scenarios. But in fact what they really mean usually is that they're doing sensitivity analysis like I just described. They take a number and vary it up and down a little bit, and that's testing a couple of scenarios. That's not what we mean. So in fact, I think the number of companies that actually do this in a thoughtful, serious, and persistent way is measured in the maybe dozens rather than hundreds.
>
> In contrast to that, our view of scenarios is based on alternative interpretations of the past. Every good scenario for the future is actually a good scenario of the past. The problem is, of course, that we don't have a single

past; we have multiple pasts. If we had a single past then we'd have one historian. We'd only need one to take the notes and add it up. But in fact we have many, many, many historians because we select our history. We select our facts, and we organize them by some kind of mental model. So there are different interpretations of the past that lead you to different interpretations or images of the future. Hence, good scenarios actually consist of three different models of the future, not the same model run three different times, where you tweak one variable or another.

I was curious to learn whether, ultimately, one of the three models was used, or whether aspects of each were incorporated as the future unfolds.

I wouldn't put it that way. I would say, Yes, it is sometimes true that one or another scenario will turn out to be more significant in a group of scenarios. That is, there may be a scenario that, for one reason or another, is more congruent with what you're planning to do. Therefore, it fits very well with, in some sense, the mental map that you're already starting with—not necessarily because you believe it is what is most likely. And then one asks the question with respect to the other scenarios: What happens if I'm wrong about that judgment? What are the consequences? How can I be prepared? Can I absorb the risk of being wrong?

I asked Schwartz what is the primary benefit of using scenarios or of taking the long view.

It's very simple—minimizing regrets. Life is full of both threats and opportunities. My view is that, particularly given the circumstances we're now experiencing, if we fail to adequately think about those in advance we'll be unprepared to recognize them and take advantage of opportunities that are emerging. And/or we'll be overwhelmed by risks that are evident out there. So we often today regret decisions in the past. We can see this acutely in business—probably in our lives, but certainly in the work of politics and business. We look back and say, "Gee, I wish we had known this" or "I wish we had thought about that." It is precisely to avoid being in that position sometime in the future looking backwards that one takes the long view.

Reperceiving the World

Another function of scenarios, according to Schwartz, is to help us "reperceive the world." I was interested to learn in more detail how he realizes this in practice with his clients.

All of us, consciously or unconsciously, have some mental maps of why and how things happen as they do. We have some set of ordering principles and rules of the game and often these are inarticulate. For some people they've actually thought about it, but most of us haven't. Those work, for the most part, reasonably well. Otherwise we would be hopelessly confused and wouldn't know how to live. So in most situations these work; therefore, we get confirmed in them.

Unfortunately—particularly in the world of business and politics and so on, where one is dealing with elaborate frameworks of policy and organization—those rules of the game that we've learned from the past are often precisely inappropriate as rules for the future. A good example of where that happened, of course, was with AT&T. The rules of the game for the monopoly era were not at all the rules of the game for the post-competition, post-breakup era. Clearly, they would have been better off if they had thought many years before about what that world might be like and how to begin the process of adaptation so as not to be compelled to adapt.

That is precisely something that has recently happened with one of the companies we work with. It is a large electric utility where, in fact, there are very large forces similar to the ones that were impacting AT&T. Part of what we did was to help them see that their basic structure and the world as they know it was going to end, that something similar to what was happening to AT&T was going to happen to them. We showed them that if they acted in a thoughtful and proactive way, they could manage that transition far better, at far less cost, and have far greater control of their future.

So they were able to reperceive what might be happening to the structure of their industry in such a way that they could actually challenge their existing world view of themselves as a kind of monopoly utility structure. They could then see how they could both transform themselves and act appropriately. And in fact, that's exactly what's happening. They're doing it. They're restructuring themselves before they're compelled to by regulators, and as a result they're actually leading the regulatory process instead of becoming its victim.

Another example of this process is from my work at Shell. One of the reasons why the oil industry, including Shell prior to 1982, believed that the price of oil was going to inevitably go up was that they thought somehow or other oil was special. It didn't follow the laws of economics. That is, if price goes up, demand goes down and supply goes up. They believed that somehow or other people have got to keep using oil no matter what the price and that people won't go looking for more even if the price goes up because what would that do to demand?

So they somehow assumed that the usual laws of supply, demand, and price didn't apply to oil. In fact, they had something they called the *backward-bending supply curve*. This was a supply curve that said the higher the price goes, the less people produce because they'll make too much money if they produce more. So they managed to construct a world view that simply reaffirmed this view: prices were going to go up, and of course, that was great because that meant you could do anything and make lots of money. So their aspirations and their world view fed each other into a massive case of self-delusion, and the whole world went with them. I believed it myself. I was just as much a victim.

So at Shell we began to ask the question, "Well, suppose it is not true that oil is special. Suppose oil is just like every other commodity? The price goes up, people use less, people go out and look for more, and eventually the supply exceeds the demand by a lot." We further noted that eventually every cartel has broken and that maybe OPEC would as well. And just suppose that, as a result, instead of behaving like some special substance with magical, noneconomic powers, oil behaved like every other commodity, and finally the price collapsed by 50 percent, which is typically what happens. Well, when we actually did this, we laid out one scenario in which exactly what they thought would happen would happen. And then we had a second scenario in which we said, "Suppose all this other stuff happens, and it becomes like a regular commodity." I said, "We don't think it's like that, of course. We think it's special. But what *if* that happens? What would we do?"

They then began to think. And as events actually began to unfold in that direction rather than in the previous direction, because they'd thought about it they could recognize it in time. And so by that act of reperception they attuned their own thinking to the signals of change in such a way that, as the changes actually unfolded, they were able to recognize them in a timely way and respond. It wasn't that they suddenly believed, "God, were we stupid before! Schwartz walked in the room and told us we were dumb, and our old world view was wrong and here's the right one." They still kept their world view at that moment, but they now had an alternate one to test against reality as the world unfolded. And as the world unfolded it tended to support the other view, and they said, "Ah, now we recognize where we're going and we can respond. We're in a different world than we thought we were."

Suspending Disbelief

One of the keys to successful use of scenarios is the suspension of disbelief, that is, getting people to believe in the plausibility of the scenarios of the future. I asked Schwartz how, in often conservative business environments, he manages to accomplish this.

I think there are three dimensions to it. One is good homework, doing good insightful research and analysis that supports your thinking. Science fiction or fantasy isn't good enough to motivate people to change. It really has to have a foundation. So good scenarios that really motivate that sense of suspension of disbelief have a lot of depth to them and meat, number one. Number two, they're told well, they're presented well, there's good storytelling, there's theater in it. And indeed, this suspension of disbelief comes from the theater. If the script is great, the acting is great, the lighting and the stage setting are great, suddenly the theater disappears and Camelot is there. At least, it feels like it for an hour or so. And then the lights come up, and you're back in reality. So good storytelling and good graphics and good imagery and an articulate presentation are very important.

I used to describe my job at Shell as a cross between secretary of state, head of the CIA, and corporate court jester. My job was to tell the people at Shell what they didn't want to hear in such an entertaining way that they didn't cut off my head. And let me tell you that that is important. It's very important, but most people tend not to take it seriously. People who are less interested in convincing others than in hearing themselves talk are less sensitive to the theatrical realities.

The final aspect of this is the nature of the multiple scenario process itself. Just take, for example, that case I cited of the Shell oil price. If I'd walked in and said, "Listen, your world view is wrong, and the price is not going to sixty dollars. In fact, it's going to sixteen dollars, and here's my forecast—take it or leave it," they would have left it. If on the other hand, I say, "Well, look, here's your world view, and I understand how it works, and here's the rules of the game as you understand them. Now here's another world view, and here's another consequence of what that might be," they can then say, "Well, ah ha! You've clearly got the right world view, and this other one is only a scenario, it's not the truth. Therefore, at least we can think about it." It doesn't force them to abandon where they are and go somewhere else instantaneously. It gives them a set of alternative lenses for perception rather than a truth that they must rediscover from a level of falsehood that they've enjoyed before. And so it is the set of scenarios *together* that create that capacity for the suspension of disbelief.

Testing the Success of a Scenario

According to Schwartz, one way to test the success of a scenario is to determine whether anyone did the "right thing" as a result of using it. I asked Schwartz if he could explain this notion further, perhaps citing some examples of successful application of scenarios.

By this we mean simply at some point in the future when things actually unfold, do clients feel like they were better off for having thought about it and did the pattern of their actions respond appropriately to the world as it unfolded? I think you can only judge that with time. In fact, my former boss, the chairman of Shell, made the argument that he would really only be able to evaluate my work in a few years, after I left the job. Which, I might add, he did; and I didn't do too badly. But the point is: it can really only be assessed with time—not overnight—after you have actually begun to respond.

In the case of the Global Business Network, it's actually fairly difficult to cite examples, in part because some of them are sufficiently new that they are "live" and it would be awkward to talk about them. They concern and affect things that companies are doing or have done recently, because we've been working with them. Let me just cite a couple of examples more in the abstract without naming names.

In the case I alluded to earlier, a utility had been focusing principally on environmental issues as the key driver of their future. By using scenarios, they recognized that, in fact, the U.S. and their region of the country were moving into a period of dramatic slowdown of growth and that lots and lots of their customers were going to be under extreme cost pressure. As a way of supporting their customers out there, they took a preemptive rate cut that has earned them an enormous amount of kudos, both from the politicians and from their customers. They now have much higher levels of customer loyalty than they would otherwise have had, because they saw the slowdown coming. They began talking about it before everybody else did, saying, "What we want to do to ease the pain that everybody's feeling is to cut our rates by 5 percent." So that was one example.

Another example was of someone in the television industry who came to recognize, in a sense, the beginning of the end of broadcast and the ultimate move of all visual images to cable rather than through the air. They began to realize two things through working with us: one, that they had a limited amount of time to make a transition to being a cable provider; two, that the value of their original franchise was going to diminish fairly rapidly. And indeed, the events began to unfold in precisely that fashion, and they were among the first to respond in transforming themselves from one kind of company into another.

The Global Business Network

I asked Schwartz what specifically the clients of the Global Business Network are seeking when they engage the firm.

Well, the companies we work with come to us for some combination of three reasons. First, they want better insight and information about the future, a wider range of perspectives than is captured by conventional wisdom. Second, they want to actually tackle real problems that they have—real issues, real decisions, real questions that they're thinking about. And third, they want to improve their capacity for thinking more thoughtfully and insightfully about the future. So our work with them involves all three elements.

On the one hand, we provide them information in a variety of forms: scenario books, meetings, interaction with people whom we think they ought to meet. In addition, we provide them help in consulting projects, working with them and actually tackling real issues. For example, we work with

Nissan on what kind of cars they should be building in the United States in the years to come. Real decisions of that nature help in coming up with their product line-up. Further, we actually help the companies develop a combination of training and facilitating processes that enable them to develop their scenarios and in the process of doing so learn how to do it. For example, we have been working in that way with Hewlett-Packard on their advanced technology strategy. We have particular packages and modules for doing all of this, but that is the basic array of things we do.

Asked how GBN organizes its work with clients, Schwartz said:

It varies a lot, but usually we have a team that is involved in interviewing some of the management people to figure out what the real issues are. They participate with them in doing some research and thinking and exploring, in other words doing some homework and preparation. The team facilitates and guides the scenario development process and helps to prepare the results afterward. I'm then often involved in communicating it within the company.

Perhaps one of the most distinguishing features about the Global Business Network is the wide range of members who are affiliated with it. These include leading academics, artists, businesspeople, and musicians. Commenting on the variety of members in GBN, Schwartz said:

As a sampling, some of our members are Danny Hillis, the inventor of the Connection Machine; Bill Joy, one of the founders of Sun Microsystems; Gary Snyder, the poet; Richard Cooper, the Harvard economist; Jeron Lanier, one of the creators of virtual reality; Alexander Singer, a television director currently doing *Star Trek: The Next Generation;* Mary Catherine Bateson, daughter of Margaret Mead and Gregory Bateson; performance artist Laurie Anderson; Bill Gibson, the science fiction writer who wrote *Neuromancer.* A great variety of people—there are eighty-five of them in all.

I asked what the rationale was behind having, for example, GBN members such as musician and artist Brian Eno participate in a conference on the future of transportation sponsored by Nissan, or rock musician Peter Gabriel serve as a consultant to AT&T.

Well, basically the notion is that there are people whose ideas, whose actions, and whose thinking is more in touch with where the world is going. Often, particularly in an era of surprise, they come from the edges rather than from the center. Furthermore, it's easy for our client companies to tap the center. It's easy for them to go to the Harvard Business School for consultants most of the time. It's easy to go to places where they can get fairly standard thinking. It's much harder for them to find insightful people out at the edges. It's not actually hard to find people out at the edges, but which ones are worth paying attention to? How do you separate freaky cultists from interesting anthropologists? A significant part of our function is to be that kind of a filter, to find some of those really interesting minds out at the outer edges who are likely to be insightful and helpful and thoughtful, rather than the crazies.

Many of our members will be actually from mainstream institutions—Michael Porter is a good example. Michael is a Harvard Business School professor, but among economists he would not be seen as part of the mainstream. He has a fairly divergent view—not that his views aren't considered widely or seriously, but he isn't in the mainstream of current economics. He offers, in fact, a fairly divergent point of view. So that's what they're really trying to get from such people.

We choose our members for any given situation by a combination of two things: the relevance of their knowledge and the chemistry between them and the company. There are some people who might be intellectually useful but who, for example, might not be helpful in the way they interact with the company. More often than not, in those cases writing is perhaps a better way of dealing with it than working face to face.

Testing Design with Scenarios

The failure to foresee the implications of design decisions is one of the leading causes of design failures. I was interested in how applicable Schwartz believes the scenario approach is to design.

Well, I'm actually an engineer by education, as you know, so in some ways it was actually my own engineering experience that led me to a kind of mindset that prepared me to undertake scenarios. As I'm sure every designer knows, there isn't only one solution to a technical problem. A pure scientist is, in a sense, looking for that one equation that absolutely captures a particular situation, and there must be only one truth. But if you're designing an airplane or a car or a new bottle, there are many design solutions to that problem. Furthermore, within each one of those, there are many, many complex trade-offs that one can make and many possible outcomes of those trade-offs, from choices of materials, to costs, to design principles applied, and so on.

Therefore, unlike science, design is inherently contingent. Design begins with the simple recognition of the fundamental malleability of the solutions to any given design problem. So I think that designers are actually well prepared to use scenarios because every designer understands that reality. I don't think anybody who designs and builds stuff would disagree with what I just said. So in that sense, they are mentally prepared.

In my view, scenarios are a way of testing a design. In my case, I learned this with airplanes in a wind tunnel. I was saying, "Okay I've got a design. What happens in use? What happens when I put it in the air now? What we want to do with an airplane is put it in the wind tunnel and test it in advance so that it doesn't crash." (Until fairly recently our mathematics was so poor there was a pretty good chance that that would happen anyway.) But at least we would try as best we could at a given scale in the wind tunnel. In a sense, scenario planning is a mental wind tunnel for design. It is asking, "What happens when I actually put this out in the world and I change the conditions of its use, making them different than I now think of them?"

As the demands and uses of designs, buildings, products, and equipment change, we must have adaptability. Therefore the question is, what kind of design principles permit that to unfold? I must say I don't have the answer to that; I wouldn't presume to answer that. But it becomes an extremely interesting question.

7 | Re-viewing Design

One of the implicit assumptions that underlies most discussions of design is the belief that the primary focus of designing is the production of form. As the preceding chapters indicate, however, formal design approaches are no longer necessarily appropriate, at least not exclusively so. They have limited applicability, for example, to information design tasks. Though there usually *is* a formal manifestation to objects such as computers, the real concern of those who will interact with them—ease of use—involves more intangible aspects, such as the design of operating systems and software.

The utility of formalist design approaches in application to more traditional tasks, such as architecture or product design, is also being questioned. There are numerous cases of award-winning designs that have failed to suit the purposes for which they were intended because too much attention was paid to form and too little to use.[1] Failures of this type are an inevitable consequence of the design process as currently conceived.

The changing nature of design tasks, with ever more emphasis on intangible qualities, requires a refocusing of the design debate away from form and on to use. British design theorist and writer John Chris Jones has spent his career re-viewing design from this point of view. He has analyzed the faulty premises that underpin traditional design practices, proposed alternative ways of viewing design tasks, and addressed the way in which these changes affect the role of the designer. The chapter that follows features a discussion with Jones in which he presents his thoughts on broadening the design process to make it more responsive to the whole of life.

John Chris Jones: Of All So Many of Us

John Chris Jones was a pioneer of the British design methods movement. From an educational background in engineering, he became involved in the then-emerging field of industrial design. Frustrated by the lack of user responsiveness in the design process, he explored the applicability of ergonomics, setting up one of the first labs in British industry devoted to the subject. Difficulties in getting the rational results of ergonomic studies incorporated into the designers' intuitive design processes led him to develop what he then termed *systematic design methods.* These were structured ways of making designing explicit so that reason and intuition could coexist in the design process, rather than having one to the exclusion of the other. Jones co-organized the first conference on design methods in 1962 and wrote *Design Methods,* which became a standard textbook, appearing first in 1970 and in revised editions in 1980 and 1992.

Jones's interest in design methods led him to leave industry for the world of education. He first headed the graduate program in Design Technology at the University of Manchester Institute of Science and Technology and later became the first Professor of Design at the British Open University. In 1974 he retired to explore more personal experiments with design, motivated in large part by the work of those in the arts, particularly the compositional approaches incorporating chance of John Cage. A number of these experiments are set out in Jones's collection of essays *designing designing,* and underlying each of them is the intention to more fully explore the question of how to make designing more human.

Portrait of John Chris Jones.
(Photograph by Jorge Glusberg, courtesy John Chris Jones)

Fail-Safe Designs

I have been greatly influenced in my thinking on design by the broad view of the subject taken by Jones. The contrast between his and more limited conceptions of the field was especially clear at a seminar held at the Institute for Contemporary Arts in London that I attended. Jones participated in a panel discussion and described the serious, and at times deadly, consequences of bad design, as reflected in the then recent Chernobyl nuclear power plant disaster in Ukraine. While the majority of the seminar was devoted to issues of style, such as the changing appearance of shopfronts in Britain, Jones addressed more fundamental design principles. I asked him about the views he expressed that night.

> I don't remember what I said about Chernobyl, but I do remember talking about the vacuum brake, which used to be fitted to steam trains, and about electrical fuses and circuit breakers as examples of fail-safe designs. The principle which these devices have in common is that they cease to function at all as soon as something goes wrong. For instance, a vacuum is used not to

apply the brakes to a train but to hold them off. If the vacuum leaks or is deliberately unsealed by the turning of an emergency handle, then the pressure of the atmosphere applies the brakes automatically. Similarly, in a fuse or a circuit breaker, the electrical current will only pass through the device if it is below a safe voltage and current. If there is a dangerous surge of electricity, either the very thin fuse wire will melt or an electromagnet, through which the current passes, will open the switch and stop the current itself. I may not have remembered the details exactly, but the principle is clear: *reverse the normal logic of operation.* Instead of designing as if accidents are not going to happen, design on the assumption that they will. Enable the design to self-regulate.

In the case of nuclear power, genetic manipulation, agrochemicals, new therapies, and drugs—any technologies that change by their presence the *systemics* (the "natural," or existing, checks and balances) of a situation—insist that the new technology is prevented from working unless, and is allowed to work only for as long as, it can be proved to be safe. Thus, the onus *to prove safety* should be placed on the designers and sponsors of the technology: the onus *to prove danger* should not be placed on consumers or potential victims, as is often the case at present. This in itself is a fail-safe practice which can be embodied in the law rather than in the hardware.

What irritates me about industrial design is that, though it grew out of protests against the inhumanity and dangers of engineering design and economic management left to themselves,[2] and though it began by adding considerations of beauty and fitness for purpose to what would otherwise have been bare engineering, it is by now insensitive to many of the human factors that are nonvisual or outside the designer's experience, as the powerful and unpredictable effects of new technologies often are. The available design skills are still inadequate to the scale of difficulties that the new technologies bring with them.[3]

You asked about the distinction between the fail-safe design of life-threatening technologies and the design of shop fronts, and of other manifestations of "designer lifestyle." At the meeting you mentioned, I was appalled by the contrast. And yet there is something to be said for the view that designing is the addition of fashionableness to otherwise unattractive or dated-looking products. Looked at anthropologically, fashion is not a triviality; it is surely one of the main manifestations of the culture, as it changes in the only way it can. As the old saying goes, "If a new idea cannot be made fashionable, it cannot be realized"—this pronouncement is perhaps a measure of fashion's importance. The difficulty is that the fashion for serious designing has disappeared for the moment.

But there is more to life than Safety First. Look at the unending variety of designs of the Swiss "Swatch," which apparently halted the decline of the traditional watch industry and must have saved many people their jobs.[4] The designs of watch faces are now as various as they are often illegible—but many people like them and feel that life is better for their presence. More alive. Yet the briefest consideration of the apparent purpose of a watch, to indicate the time, would condemn many fashionable watch faces as failures. However, thinking of life as a whole, what *is* the purpose of a watch? Not only to let you know the time (perhaps more frequently than you need to know it for the good of your mental health or peace of mind) but also to enjoy buying the object, wearing it, matching it to whatever else you choose to wear today, *to be the figure that you like to think you are.* Where I quarrel with postmodern design is not in its widening of the idea of purpose to include the nonfunctional, the presence of the thing *as object,* as part of the "art of living"—to use an old phrase. But when all this is done at the expense of the invisible, the nonvisual, and when it diminishes the idea of what it is to be human—those are my main concerns. I guess that your other questions will enable me to describe more exactly these elements of *intangible design.*

Blaming the Operator

I asked Jones to elaborate on his view that most accidents purportedly caused by "human error" can actually be traced back to the designer.

> Throughout my life I have been angered by the policy of blaming the operator for crashes and other disasters of technology which are entirely predictable at the design stage, or earlier. To attribute a technical failure to human error is often to misunderstand the nature of human skill.
>
> For instance, if you attempt the simple task of pressing a button every time a particular light comes on, you will miss seeing the light (or you will press the switch when no light comes on) about once in every five hundred attempts, no matter how hard you try not to make mistakes. Furthermore, you will be unconscious that you made the mistake, because your nervous system, your *link with reality,* does not operate continuously. It's intermittent. It suffers from "internal blinks." What we take to be smooth and continuous knowledge or awareness of our surroundings is rather like our vision of the TV screen or our reading of a book: a mere sampling, through eye movements and memory, of what is actually before us. The rest is inferred.
>
> When you are unskilled, you notice this, for instance, in learning to drive a car. As a learner you may miss seeing pedestrians, traffic lights, other cars. You may even fail to look at the road ahead at all in your conscious efforts to get your hands and feet to synchronize in operating the gearshift in conjunction with the clutch and the accelerator. But when you are skilled, you can drive safely for miles without noticing what you are doing while simultaneously carrying on a conversation and keeping your subconscious attention several hundred yards ahead to anticipate the actions of yourself and other road users before they happen. In this way, the skilled nervous system operates *automatically* (i.e., unconsciously). So, on the rare occasions when the

skilled nervous system *unconsciously fails,* it is wrong to blame the driver. If he or she were required to be conscious of every action, car driving would have to be slowed down to the pace and hesitancy of the learner. It would be like "working to rule" in a strike, only worse. It wouldn't even be safer.

Most of this has been known for fifty years or more: it is the central know-how of ergonomics, although, if you attend only to those static, anthropometric mannequins, you might never guess it. There has yet to be a serious attempt to reorganize industrial life on the basis of this dynamic knowledge. If this were done, then not only would the responsibility for accidents be placed where it belongs (in the decisions of those who introduce a new technology and who benefit from it) but the mechanical tempo of industrial life (so obviously mismatched to the many rhythms of the body, from breathing and heartbeat to sleeping/waking and gestation) would be transformed. People would come first and technologies second—or even last. The resulting life forms could be marvelous. Artifice might resemble nature in its varieties and rhythms, and the stress of artificial living might be gone.

Traffic Automation Case Study

A characteristic product of Jones's more systemic view of designing is his proposal for an automated traffic system, first conceived in 1959.[5]

> The central point of this proposal was to reject the present mixture of cars, buses, taxis, roads, traffic lights, traffic police, car parks, traffic meters, and so on as a hopeless failure, with its notorious "insoluble" problems of congestion, parking, and traffic accidents, not to mention pollution and the attempts to solve the problem by adding urban highways and the multistory car parks, which create "the concrete jungle."
>
> I took the first three of these problems of high-density traffic and asked myself if there were other kinds of crowded movement in which such problems do not occur. What came to mind were the movements of swarms of bees, flights of migrating birds, and the complex movements of people walking in all directions across a railway plaza without slowing down, without colliding with each other, and without clogging the space with empty vehicles.
>
> Why, I asked myself, are people in road vehicles so unable to travel smoothly and safely in high density when birds, insects, and people on their feet can do so easily? The answer, I thought, is information. The professions then responsible for city traffic (civil engineers, police, lawmakers, and vehicle designers—this was in 1959) were each trying to solve the problem piecemeal, using the inappropriate methods of pouring concrete, enforcing laws, and making feeble attempts to reduce the size and increase the parkability, but not the number, of cars. The right solution, I felt sure, was to give to each driver and vehicle sufficient information and freedom of action to be

able to steer clear of congestion before it became excessive and to free everyone from parking difficulties by making each vehicle automatic enough to find its own way to the next people wanting to move, once its present occupants had got out. The automatic control of vehicles, through a magnetic tape embedded in the road, would remove the need for traffic lights and would make traffic collisions almost impossible. Car parks could be eliminated, and the utilization of vehicles could rise from say 5 percent, as at present, to perhaps 90 percent, as each vehicle would be moving most of the time, thus freeing up most of the curb space for getting in and out wherever you wish and reducing the need to manufacture so many cars in the first place.

The result of this thinking was a scheme for complete traffic automation which could be introduced in easy stages over the twenty years from 1959 to 1979 and which would gradually reduce the main features of the traffic problem to nearly nil. The scheme assumed that the users of cars, taxis, and buses could be persuaded to abandon their present vehicles for small automatic cars and minibuses which could be called to any phone or (transformed) parking meter, from which the traveler indicated his or her position and destination. Each traveler would be given an expected arrival time at destination, depending on the density of traffic, and if this was excessive would have the choice of canceling the request until a quicker journey became possible. In this way, I proposed to provide each of the millions of minds, presently immobilized by information scarcity, the means to use its own intelligence, as in the case of birds, bees, and people walking on a piazza. This is what I call true decentralization or constructive anarchy. I think control from the center is barbaric. It's useful only in emergencies.

There's more to this scheme, but I think I've said enough to show why I reject altogether the "bad design" of city traffic, and indeed of industrial life as we know it, and why the kinds of solution I seek, though so beautifully fitting in theory, are so very difficult to realize. They cut against the vested interest of each of us in our specialized, paid, or sanctified roles as car owner, car worker, civil engineer, policeman, lawyer, parking attendant, taxi driver, bus driver, and so on. And they call for a scale of thinking and of collective responsibility that is far beyond what is encouraged in the culture as it is. Yes, it's courage we need, the courage to *tackle the whole*—but without imposing our preconceptions—and to live out the probably amazing consequences of doing so *decentrally* and *without control*. "I made it without an idea," said Marcel Duchamp, referring to *The Large Glass,* his central work. What I'm describing is, I think, art, the art of technology, unthreatening and free, the spirit of the time. Why not?

However, all is not hopeless. Since 1959, when the traffic scheme became *technically* feasible (using electronics then being developed for the space program),[6] many electronic fragments of the scheme have appeared piecemeal: the linking of traffic lights to permit tidal flow, automatic control of distance between vehicles, electronic maps in cars to show congestion, parking places, and so on. Unfortunately, these bits and pieces are being allied with ideas such as road pricing, automatic surveillance, and central control, none of which show the equality and trust possible when such subsolutions are linked together in a cybernetic and democratic "antiplan" for collective intelligence, such as *true* traffic automation allows. Again: the need to *change our minds.* When will it happen? And where is the selfless kind of "negative leadership" that could make it possible? I believe they're to be seen in the work of artists like John Cage and Joseph Beuys and in the unspoken thoughts of many.

Intangible Designs

Jones has done a wide range of work addressing the emerging concept of intangible design, and I was interested to learn more of the way he approaches these projects.

You ask how do I *approach* projects such as traffic automation, car seat comfort, trying to teach this view of design, devising a book of design methods, or my recent attempts at "improving" theatre and novel-writing by attempting to change the conventions of realism? In that sentence is a selection of my favorite "designs," intangible as they may appear. I could try to tell how I approached designs with more physical presence, such as "the car of the future," eating utensils, computer interfaces, and so on, but that would be on a smaller scale, less relevant to what I've been saying.

Goodness knows if I can find words to say what's common to these attempts at *intangible design,* but now you've asked me I'd like to try. As I think back to these attempts, I notice that they all arose from a single strategy or method.

My method in doing work of this kind is simply this: to put myself *at the receiving end.* For traffic automation, I first imagined myself going through all the motions of a person who is traveling in city traffic, whether by car, by taxi, by bus, or on foot. At each significant point or "obstacle"—deciding to go on a trip, getting in the car, waiting for a bus, getting caught in congestion, and so on—I wrote down what is good or bad about the experience.[7] Then, when the comments seem complete, I slowly devise an ideal standard of experience for each event or obstacle. As I do this, I record in a different part of my notes the various connected ideas or "breakthroughs" which occur in my mind as I contemplate the possibility of a city without congestion, a car seat without discomfort, a form of design teaching that does not perpetuate the past, a book of design methods that reaches beyond the ideas of the methodologists (including myself), or a kind of play or novel that takes account of the presence of the audience, of readers, of the world outside the theatre or book, and of the sounds and shapes of the words themselves as things, not messages or commandments to believe.

From the imposed to the adaptive J. Chris Jones

...book, clock, phone, TV, computer, credit card, game, pill and spaceflight. The soft technologies, or some of them. Not that names of the products, the objects, gives the feel of them. That is more evident in the verbs, the processes : printing, publishing, reading, 'what time is it?', phoning, watching TV, computing, programming, credit-rating, cash-dispensing, playing space invaders, designing the process. What is it that these have in common ? Most obviously, I'd say, it is that they are non-mechanical, depending not on wheels, gears, pistons, rivets, or heat engines, but on electric power, low currents, complex circuits, minute components, invisible processes, relativities (in place of absolute standards), and on finding external analogues and processes fast and delicate enough to be matched to the operations of the eye, the ear, the brain or any other organ of the body.

To cross the apparent divide between the poetic and the natural, the thing and the thought, the machine and 'the human' (as we so distantly call ourselves, seen theoretically). Nothing is outside the range of these new technologies, these extensions of our bodyminds, though much of what is printed, phoned, broadcast, bought, or otherwise done within and through them, is cut down to the predictable, the range of what is common to all of us in millions. That has been the first step : equality, an even standard, which began as the idealistic spreading of the material basis of what had been aristocratic life to nearly everyone, and has by now become 'the plastic world', the homo-genising, the reduction of everything not only to what can be sold at a profit but to a level of security, materialism, and 'inhumanity' that excludes the differences that make us persons, not mere numbers. The functional product, the means-to-an-end, no longer seen or conceived as what it is, as what every object is : a part, a piece, of the earth, the miracle, the mind.

John Chris Jones, excerpt from *From the Imposed to the Adaptive* (Antwerp: Verhaert, 1994), 5.

Jones's writing is included to illustrate his views on intangible designing.

Well, I don't know if that description is enough to let anyone share or copy the experiences I'm trying to describe, but to me it's very clear: I approach such questions simply by studying what it is like to experience *things as they are,* and then I try to design a new version which is completely free of all that I find unpleasant, regardless of any resistance to changing the status quo—and, I hope, despite my preconceptions.

I try to put people first and organizations last. That's the only way to go about it, it seems to me, if designing is not to be forever tied to supporting "what is wrong" and is to become the means through which the culture itself can evolve, can self-organize, can change and grow. This is not a matter of self-expression but of looking outward and seeing what we produce as itself becoming a part of nature, the sublime creation, or whatever it is.

Beyond the Individual Object

I asked Jones if there were specific designs that irritated him and provoked him to pursue the direction he's taken.

For the moment I can't think of any. What seems wrong to me is that designers are restricted to designing single objects when what needs changing is the design process itself, and with it the way of life. No amount of change to the physical design of cars is going to solve the traffic problem. No changes in the design of jobs are going to solve the so-called problem of unemployment.[8] No changes to the design of schools and colleges, or even to their curricula, are going to undo the basic error of education—namely, that it forces all the youngest and liveliest people to do obediently what their elders tell them until the age of about twenty-five, when what they really need is the know-how to take over the shaping of life while they still have the energy and imagination to do it. How about *that* as an alternative to drugs and crimes of violence? And no conceivable changes to broadcasting—apart from getting rid of the professional broadcasters—will release everyone from the passivity of becoming "couch potatoes," as we now have the nerve to call ourselves in the inactive role we nearly all assume for about twenty hours a week in front of TV screens.

So my answer to this question is: forget products, forget industrial design in the form we know it now, and do something about the hopelessness of relying on professionals and specialists and all kinds of police persons to change the culture as a whole. What happens at present is just a mismatching, a total mismatching, of what we do (designing, making, distributing, and discarding products, physical and economic, for the narrow motive of economic security alone) to what we are (almost a new species of beings if you include our technologies, our extrabodily extensions, our collective presence as and in "the virtual world").

I feel that it is not the bad design of individual products that leads me to this near-total *condemnation of everything*—laughable or even cranky as that may sound—but the dreadful, accumulated sensations and experiences of trying to live amongst the disconnected and discordant actions and perceptions that constitute the actual lives of everyone today, even the so-called leaders. To participate in this nonsense is a crime in itself. Yet what can we do?

On a recent journey, for example, I sat on a train that was very nearly too bumpy to write in, on a seat that failed to support my aching back, after a sea journey that was delayed for two hours due to a broken fuel line (the reason for our delay was kept from us until the journey was over; some of us must have been wondering anxiously, remembering the ferryboat *Estonia,* which had recently sunk with nearly a thousand passengers). The electromagnetic interference in the train was so great that it is nearly impossible to listen to radio. There was no connecting boat train, so we were put onto a local train that stopped everywhere. There was no one to meet us at the station, no one who could tell us how long we'd have to wait—only five TV screens displaying outdated train times.

But I don't want to sound like an unlucky and disgruntled traveler who is forgetting all the times when trains and boats did run to time and when the journey was pleasant. What I'm trying to say is that the whole of our industrial way of life, every part of it, is pervaded by bad microexperiences which everyone has grown to accept as inevitable, from imposed noise and polluted air and junk food to poor seating, queues, bad access, repetitive work, unhelpful officials, unsafe and congested transportation, aggressive advertising, commercialized news media, tedious TV, and clumsy and insensitive software, not to mention the far worse conditions in the poorer countries upon which all this misconceived materialism depends. . . . I could go on and on and on.

Why do we put up with it? Where is the modern substitute for the joys of pure air, of autonomous living in natural surroundings, qualities that still attract us to the unattainable idea of a life in the wilds for everyone? When is the improvement of the pattern of life as a whole—as each person experiences it day by day, minute by minute—going to become the subject, the operational unit, the aim and purpose of creative endeavor? The notion and existence of industrial design can be a small help in all this, but I fear it's lost the impetus to aim for *higher things*. What I've been driven to do in my work, modest as it is in relation to these aims, is to try nevertheless, here and there, *to design at the scale of life, the scale of mind itself* while refusing to act at the scale of its hopelessly disconnected fragments. Easy to say, difficult to do. Perhaps impossible at the moment.

I was curious, in terms of these comments, to learn how Jones defined good and bad design.

Well, initially I'd prefer not to define these terms because *thinking in opposites* could be a way to perpetuate, not to escape, the dualism that pervades industrial culture and is possibly a cause of what is wrong. If I try to define *good design*, what comes to my mind is a new kind of industrial living that is organized decentrally, a multiple culture in which every single person is a unique norm or center around which everything is organized dynamically, moment by moment. Computers can make this possible if we give them the chance—technology can be reorganized and changed to enable the apparent miracle of multiplicity to happen, person by person, event by event. Such a technology would not simply be used to further the interests of owners and managers and all of us as specialists (all of us as instruments of abstract economic goals); it would not force everything to fit the administrative convenience of the oversimplified life as seen by "central control." According to this view of things, bad design comes of diminished and crushing images of what it is to be a person, the dumb idea that the purpose of living is only to produce and to consume and to do as you're told and to enjoy the incentives.

People-Dependent Technology

Jones coined the term *people-dependent technology* to describe this relationship, in which people come first and technology is subservient.

That is a new term, for which as yet I can think of no examples—it is my current hope. What I envisage is that, instead of designing everything (and particularly computer software) on the assumption that people are going to behave like machines—that is, without feeling love, hatred, anticipation, intuition, imagination, and so on, the very qualities we associate with being human—we design everything on the assumption that people are not heartless imbeciles but marvelously capable, given the chance, each and every one. I'd like to see machines, systems, environments of all kinds designed in such a way that if they are to work well, everyone who uses or inhabits them will be challenged to act at her or his best, with no built-in obstacles to doing that. The main obstacle to this at present is not so much machines and technical processes per se as the presence of our other selves, as paid professionals, "protecting" every one of us from our mechanical or overspecialized selves and enforcing rules of behavior and design which assume that users know nothing and producers know all.

If you analyze any professional job, from doctoring to policing, from teaching to designing products, I think you will find that professional knowhow has two parts. There is the rational part, which can be embodied in a book or in a piece of software, and there is the intuitive part, which can only be learned in practice. In my picture of *people-dependent technology*, all professional jobs are eliminated. The rational know-how of the professions is made available to users directly, through screens, keyboards, and the like, while the intuitive skills are learned by the users themselves through trial and error and through simulation more than through instruction by teachers.

The resultant "cybernetic utopia" is something I'd like to see attempted immediately through the medium of experimental cities, through imaginative instead of threatening movies, and through a complete reversal of education away from logical know-how and towards colloquial skills.[9] If it were to happen, I'd expect to see each person composing the human or colloquial parts of her or his own education, medical care, security, government, food, sport, reading matter, entertainment, and so on, with the rational parts being provided by an autonomous automation that has been freed of professional bias and control. The implications of this are, I'm sure, enormous, and I hope to spend the next part of my life exploring what they could be.

The change to this kind of thinking, to this "softecnical" approach, after several centuries of thinking of people as if they are mechanisms, is vast, but it's already beginning. That is why now I am not working on design and technology directly but am attempting fictions, plays, and other such forms or genres in the name of design. I believe that before we can hope for all this, we have to change our culture. We have to remake ourselves, our mental pictures of what we are.

And what is life if full of care

We have no time to stand and stare.[10]

(I'm thinking here of pastoral or preindustrial living.) Designing has already left its narrow basis in things, in exclusively physical products, and has begun to spread itself to everything, no longer as a way of imposing on the many but as a way of listening to each other and to ourselves. "The composer becomes a listener," as John Cage says.[11] Designers, too?

John Chris Jones, excerpt from "1980 Edition: A Review of New Topics," in _Design Methods_, 2d ed. (New York: Van Nostrand Reinhold, 1992), xxvi.

---

xxxvi
POST-MODERNISM
Suddenly, in architecture and the arts, the modern age (the time of progress, functionalism, abstraction, etc) is over. Instead we have a new nostalgia, a revival of the past, even of the recent modernist past. At first sight this seems like a loss of nerve, a flight from the present. But, behind the apparent weakness, joke-yness, of post-modernist fashions, is, I think, a new wisdom, hitherto absent from the thought of our time: the notion that progress, and 'the new', need no longer <u>replace</u> the old. What exists is good, in its own way; there is no need to destroy it. The new and the old can exist together, side-by-side.

CONTEXTUAL DESIGNING
It is unlikely that 'design participation', the sharing of the process of design with those affected by its results, will make much difference until the nature of designing is itself changed, eg by transferring <u>responsibility</u> from designers to makers and users. Such a change is happening spontaneously in computing, where soft-ware designers are also the makers, and can be users too. It has happened intentionally in music, where some composers have given up control of the sounds to be heard when performers react to scores which do not indicate notes, or tempo, but perhaps only duration, type of instrument, or state of mind. 'The composer becomes a listener' as John Cage says. So does the performer. And the aud-ience has to be far more creative than it was before. 'But this is not music' say the critics. It is, if you accept that we are cap-able of changing our minds, of learning to enjoy sounds which form-erly we'd have ignored, beauties unexpected. I believe that this big shift in the responsibilities of composers, performers, and audiences is a good model of what is needed now in design: a change <u>from</u> the specifying of geometry, physical form, <u>to</u> the making of a context, a situation, in which it is possible for others, for us all as users, makers, imaginers, to determine the geometry our-selves. It requires a new tradition, a new sensitivity, and much learning by everyone.

1 2 3 4 5 6 7 8 9 0
q w e r t y u i o p
a s d f g h j k l ;
z x c v b n m , . ½

Conclusion

This project began as an examination of innovative design approaches and an inquiry into the nature of good and bad design. On the basis of my interviews, however, it became clear that a more fundamental question must be asked as the end of the twentieth century draws near: What *is* design, and how is it now best done? The answer to this varies with each participant, and in some cases their views are directly contradictory to one another, but what is shared is the belief that designing is a deeper and broader process than is conventionally supposed. After conducting my conversations, I concluded that there were seven key design considerations that are focused on to a greater or lesser extent by all of the participants in their work. These are Infusing Meaning, Increasing Scope, Involving Users, Enhancing Perception, Considering Context, Thinking Strategically, and Re-viewing Design.

Infusing Meaning

This first consideration, Infusing Meaning, is intended to help designers avoid the alienating quality that is characteristic of much modern design. Michael McCoy's Interpretive Design approach, for example, is based on the premise that design should be done with the intention of making the purpose and use of objects or environments clear. Through use of a formal language based on recognizable metaphors, McCoy's work, and that of his students, attempts to communicate to laypeople as well as designers. Use of the interpretive design approach enables designers to go beyond the merely competent in order to create a rich, context-dependent relationship between objects and people.

Increasing Scope

Ironically, Increasing Scope entails not just looking at design more broadly but also addressing tasks in more detail. Though operating in very different ways, Daniel

161

Weil and Frank Duffy both emphasize the importance of a new, encompassing form of knowledge-based design professionalism. At the largest scale, designers should transcend the limitations of discipline-based designing and take responsibility for real issues, such as the evolution of the building stock as whole over time. At the other extreme, designers should recognize the need for more technical specialization and detailed attention to the making, and not just the planning, of their work.

Involving Users

Involving Users is central to the work of many of those who were included in this book. The importance is clear: No one can know more about the activities and aspirations of design users than they themselves. Laypeople, however, are often unable to clearly express these ideas owing to a lack of visual training and because so much of their behavior is out of conscious awareness. Lucien Kroll has tackled the difficult task of involving users in the design of his buildings and town plans. As Kroll rightly notes, truly democratic architecture and design can only be realized through a meaningful collaboration with those to be affected by designing.

Enhancing Perception

When producing complex multifunction or information-based designs, it is necessary to systematically address the many different facets of user experience. Both Clino Trini Castelli and Edwin Schlossberg have made the enhancement of perception a central focus of their design processes. Castelli has traditionally addressed the "soft," intangible qualities of space more than tangible form. Schlossberg's firm, in its design of museums, other learning environments, and interfaces, has aimed to "create conversations," or foster meaningful interactions, between people and the built environment. With these approaches the built environment is seen as a tool to perception, rather than simply as an object in space.

Considering Context

It is important to explicitly consider the social context in which design will be situated in any case, but with information technology this is especially critical. Kiyoshi Sakashita, Donald Norman, and John Seely Brown have all addressed this issue in their work. Sakashita's *humanware* concept, for example, challenges traditional hardware-driven product development, replacing it with an approach in which technology is tailored to the cultural and psychological needs of those who will use it. Donald Norman has clearly articulated the psychological principles that underpin people's use of design and, more recently, has begun to address the organizational changes needed to bring about truly user-responsive design in the corporate context. John Seely Brown stresses that design should be user-*centering,* that is, designed in such a way that it "brings people in" to an understanding of its purpose and use. As the work of these three people makes clear, in order to create a truly effective design, the cultural context, or "social web," in which design is situated must be understood in depth and made the basis for design.

Thinking Strategically

Thinking Strategically is, in a sense, related to Increasing Scope. It differs, however, in that it concerns, for the most part, the larger context within which formal designing takes place. Approaches based on strategic thinking enable clients to determine what their needs for design are and what the long-term effects of their decisions are likely to be. John Thackara's *cultural engineering* concept, for example, implicitly acknowledges that though designing is often viewed as an individualistic activity, there is always a larger framework of client needs and expectations that must be addressed if design is to satisfy all concerned. Larry Keeley and his colleagues use the Strategic Design Planning approach to analyze emerging trends in the culture and to gain an understanding of what people do in their daily lives. On the basis of this research, Doblin Group works with clients to create radically new products and services that, very often, transform the nature of their clients' industries. Peter Schwartz's scenario method is predicated on the belief that change in the world is the rule and not the exception. Use of his method allows designers to consider this eventuality and, in turn, to make their designs flexible enough to accommodate the likely changes in use that will occur over time. These three strategic thinking techniques provide ways of understanding and addressing the many competing interests that must be resolved in order to do design successfully.

Re-viewing Design

When Re-viewing Design in terms of the work presented in this book, it becomes clear that, in application to many of today's most urgent design tasks, traditional approaches have lost whatever relevance they may once have had. The scale of design is no longer that of the individual design object or even the isolated system. As John Chris Jones points out, designing must now take place at the scale of life itself, with all its complexities and contradictions. Though it is not at all clear what the long-term implications of this change in scale and orientation of design are,

Jones *is* very clear about the attitude that designers should adopt in the face of it—the designer, like some avant-garde composers, should *become a listener.*

Though present in different forms, attentive listening seems to underpin all of the work included in this book. Rather than imposing their own ideas, those interviewed seek inspiration in what is real, connected, and grounded in the world. They recognize the importance of understanding the context in which their work will be situated and involving those to be affected by designing in the process. Instead of creating art objects fixed in space, their work is seen a tool through which to foster a conversation between people and design over time.

Through their work the project participants show the way forward to a new, very different, and much more user-oriented approach to design. Metaphorically, if the work of those interviewed for this book is underpinned by listening and hearing, then mainstream approaches are predicated on telling and imposing. What is proposed here is to make the monologue a dialogue, not just between designers and users but also between designs and those who interact with them. This reperception of the world has already begun and promises to transform the nature of design practice.

Endnotes

Introduction

1. Cited in Dirk J. Stratton, "Design Defined," *Aldus Magazine* 4, no. 1 (November/December 1992): 92.

2. John Thackara, communication to Wendy Lochner, 9 December 1992.

3. See discussion in Mattys Levy and Mario Salvadori, *Why Buildings Fall Down: How Structures Fail* (New York: W. W. Norton, 1992), 109–20.

4. See discussion in ibid., 57–67.

5. John Chris Jones, *Design Methods,* 2d ed. (New York: Van Nostrand Reinhold, 1992), 3.

6. This theme is central to all of Jones's recent writings. A good collection of them is contained in John Chris Jones, *designing designing* (London: ADT Press, 1991).

7. Donald Norman, conversation with author.

1. Infusing Meaning

1. Alix M. Freedman, "Forsaking the Black Box: Designers Wrap Products in Visual Metaphors," *Wall Street Journal,* 26 March 1987, 39.

2. Involving Users

1. Andrew J. King, review of *Redefining Designing* by C. Thomas Mitchell, *Journal of Design History* 7, no. 1 (1994): 63.

4. Enhancing Perception

1. Le Corbusier [Charles-Édouard Jeanneret], *Towards a New Architecture,* trans. Frederick Etchells (London: Architectural Press, 1927), 7.

5. Considering Context

1. Quoted in Dick Powell, "The Human Road Ahead," *Design* 407 (November 1982): 38.

2. Quoted in Christopher Parkes, "Marketing and Advertising: Where Design Is Given a High Profile," *Financial Times,* 14 August 1986, sec. 1, p. 18.

3. "Essential Design: Sharp Design Concept," unpublished diagram, Sharp Corporation, Osaka.

4. Kiyoshi Sakashita, "Corporate Design for the Twenty-first Century," *Sharp News* (undated publication of the Sharp Corporation, Osaka), photocopy.

5. Quoted in Parkes, "Marketing and Advertising."

6. "Ubiquitous Computing" (N.p.: Xerox, 1993).

7. Mark Weiser, "The Computer for the Twenty-first Century," *Scientific American* 265, no. 3 (September 1, 1991): 94–95, 98–102, 104.

6. Thinking Strategically

1. John Chris Jones, *Design Methods*, 2d ed. (New York: Van Nostrand Reinhold, 1992), xxv.

7. Re-Viewing Design

1. See, for example, the discussion in my first book, C. Thomas Mitchell, *Redefining Designing: From Form to Experience* (New York: Van Nostrand Reinhold, 1993), xi–xxiii.

2. I am thinking here of John Ruskin, William Morris, and others whose protests against the brutalities of the coal and iron phase of industrialization led eventually, through the actions of the German Werkbund and the like, to the appearance of industrial design as a new profession of "visual humanizers," still not fully accepted or understood and perhaps not always aware of their own significance as changers of the culture. *J.C.J.*

3. One of the good things about modernism, presently under a cloud, is that it gave designers and others in a position to innovate the cultural impetus or encouragement to make changes to the culture itself as well as to its accepted parts. To insist on fail-safe designing is to go outside the existing culture if you ask for more than the economic constraints allow. The recent switch to the superficialities of the "designer lifestyle" or of design as trivia may sacrifice this most valuable ability of the culture to redesign itself, to transcend its own defects when these become evident, to extend to the artificial world the quality of spontaneous evolution. Could the refusal of serious designing be a cultural death wish? Whatever happened to the Romans? *J.C.J.*

4. If you think jobs are good. I don't. It is the business of design as I see it to look beyond such limited ideas as job creation to the wider idea of living without work. *J.C.J.*

5. For a more detailed discussion of the traffic system proposal, see "the future of breathing," in John Chris Jones, *designing designing* (London: ADT Press, 1991), xvi–xli, and "System Transformation" in idem., *Design Methods,* 2d ed. (New York: Van Nostrand Reinhold, 1992), 316–24. *J.C.J.*

6. I thought in those days that if something was technically feasible, it was socially feasible as well. But I still believe that we are all capable of changing our minds. *J.C.J.*

7. This is what, elsewhere (e.g., in the book *Notes and Plays* [London: Spectacular Diseases, forthcoming]), I call *existentia*. As I turn away from specific products and towards rethinking the conventions of theater, fiction, broadcasting, computing, virtual reality, and other such forms of modern life, I find this more and more the way to proceed, to get outside the imposed culture. The essential skill is that of listening to the chatter of the mind, the tiny thoughts and passing feelings that we normally discount and censor. *J.C.J.*

8. I just can't see unemployment as a problem at all: wasn't freedom from the bondage of work the very purpose of using machines in the first place, at least in the minds of their inventors? And isn't unemployment also the distinguishing mark of the child, the freeman, the aristocrat, the politician, the poet, the artist, the lover, the romantic, the saint—all the types of people from whom we can learn the way to liberate ourselves

from the false necessities of the utilitarian world that our recent ancestors foisted upon us but which contradicts so many of the better notions of what it is to really live? "Consider the lilies of the field, they toil not neither do they spin." Surely, it's time to aspire again to such considerations as these if we are to rise to the occasion of our inventions, at last, and not remain forever in the self-imposed slavery of mechanized specialization? Yes indeed, I'm losing my patience! *J.C.J.*

9. By this I mean the spontaneous skill by which a baby learns not only how to speak but how to live in the culture, without conscious knowledge of grammar or rules or any teaching by specialists. A useful measure of "good design" is whether or not the thing can be used colloquially, with "zero learning," as I've called it in the past, using only one's existing skills and know-how. The more profound aspects of existence are those that are learned and communicated in this way. In an emergency, or under heavy stress, these are what remain. My Welsh accent is more me than is this, and it could be the last thing to go. *J.C.J.*

10. W. H. Davies. This simple poem and his *Autobiography of a Supertramp* seem to me so central to everything decentral! *J.C.J.*

11. To be surprised at the result—that is how John Cage says he composed his music, not knowing how it would sound. See *John Cage, Writer,* ed. Richard Kostelanetz (New York: Limelight Editions, 1993), 246. *J.C.J.*

Bibliography

Preface

Brand, Stewart. 1994. *How buildings learn: What happens after they're built.* New York: Viking Penguin.

Mitchell, C. Thomas. 1993. *Redefining designing: From form to experience.* New York: Van Nostrand Reinhold.

Introduction

Blake, Peter. 1977. *Form follows fiasco.* Boston: Little, Brown.

Caplan, Ralph. 1982. *By design: Why there are no locks on the bathroom doors in the Hotel Louis XIV and other object lessons.* New York: St. Martin's Press.

Jones, John Chris. 1992. *Design methods.* 2d ed. New York: Van Nostrand Reinhold.

————. 1991. *designing designing.* London: ADT Press.

Levy, Mattys, and Mario Salvadori. 1992. *Why buildings fall down: How structures fail.* New York: W. W. Norton.

Petroski, Henry. 1992. *To engineer is human: The role of failure in successful design.* New York: Vintage Books.

Stratton, Dirk J. 1992. Design defined. *Aldus Magazine* 4, no. 1 (November–December): 92.

1. Infusing Meaning

Venturi, Robert. 1966. *Complexity and contradiction in architecture.* New York: Museum of Modern Art.

Venturi, Robert, Denise Scott Brown, and Steven Izenour. 1972. *Learning from Las Vegas.* Cambridge, Mass.: MIT Press.

Michael McCoy: Interpretive Design

Aldersey-Williams, Hugh. 1988. Object Culture. *Blueprint* 49 (July–August): 38–39.

Aldersey-Williams, Hugh, et al. 1990. *Cranbrook design: The new discourse.* New York: Rizzoli.

Braybrook, Susan. 1985. Cranbrook at sixty. *Print* 39, no. 6 (November–December): 77–89, 124, 126.

Freedman, Alix M. 1987. Forsaking the black box: Designers wrap products in visual metaphors. *Wall Street Journal,* 26 March, p. 39.

Krohn, Lisa, and Michael McCoy. 1989. Beyond beige: Interpretive design for the post-industrial age. *Design Issues* 5, no. 2 (Spring): 112–23.

McCoy, Michael. 1993. Design and the new mythology. In *The edge of the millennium: An international critique of architecture, urban planning, product and communication design,* edited by Susan Yelavich, 132–38. New York: Whitney Library of Design.

2. Increasing Scope

Daniel Weil: New Design Territories

Dormer, Peter. 1992. Lines of thought. *Design* 518 (February): 44–45.

Paz, Octavio. 1970. *Marcel Duchamp; or, The castle of purity.* Translated by Donald Gardner. London: Cape Goliard Press.

Poynor, Rick. 1986. Daniel Weil: Illuminating the object. *Designers' Journal* 22 (November): 62–65.

———. 1988. Form follows idea. *Blueprint* 49 (July–August): 32–35.

Thackara, John, ed. 1986. *New British design.* London: Thames and Hudson.

Weil, Daniel. 1985. *Light box.* London: Architectural Association.

Francis Duffy: The Choreography of Change

Becker, Franklin, et al. 1985. *Orbit-2: Executive overview.* Norwalk, Conn.: Harbinger Group.

Charles, Prince of Wales. 1989. *A vision of Britain: A personal view of architecture.* London: Doubleday.

Duffy, Francis. 1992. *The changing workplace.* Edited by Patrick Hannay. London: Phaidon Press.

Duffy, Francis, and Alex Henney. 1989. *The changing city.* London: Bulstrode Press.

Duffy, Francis, Andrew Laing, and Vic Crisp. 1993. *The responsible workplace: The redesign of work and offices.* Oxford: Butterworth Architecture.

Duffy, Francis, et al. 1983. *Information technology and office design: The Orbit study.* Edited by Maryanne Chandor. London: Orbit.

3. Involving Users

King, Andrew J. 1994. Review of *Redefining designing* by C. Thomas Mitchell. *Journal of Design History* 7, no. 1: 61–63.

Lucien Kroll: Contemporaneous Architecture

Blundell-Jones, Peter. 1992. Ecolonia. *The Architectural Review* 190 (March): 64–69.

Kamin, Blair. 1993. Results of the Chicago Tribune Architecture Competition for Public Housing. *Chicago Tribune.* 20 June, final edition, Arts, p. 4.

Kroll, Lucien. 1975. Soft zone. *Architectural Association Quarterly* 7, no. 4: 48–59.

———. 1981. Our friends the rationalists. *Architectural Design* 51: 91–95.

———. 1986. Laroche-Clermault. Translated by Anne Fougeron. *Places* 3, no. 4: 37–45.

———. 1987. *The architecture of complexity.* Translated by Peter Blundell Jones. Cambridge, Mass.: MIT Press.

———. 1987. *Buildings and projects.* Translated by Joseph Masterson. New York: Rizzoli.

4. Enhancing Perception

Le Corbusier [Charles-Édouard Jeanneret]. 1927. *Towards a new architecture.* Translated by Frederick Etchells. London: Architectural Press.

Clino Trini Castelli: Design *Primario*

Cohen, E. 1983. Best in the Mart: Herman Miller: designed by Clino Castelli and Tom Singel. *Interior Design* 54, no. 12 (December): 188–91.

Color and user interface—Clino Castelli. 1991. *Axis* 39 (spring): 88.

Gibb, Julian. 1985. Soft: An appeal to common senses. *Design* 433 (January): 27–29.

Herman Miller: Color system for systems furniture. 1983. *American Fabrics and Fashions* 129: 43–50.

Thackara, John. 1985. Designing without form. *Design* 440 (August): 38–39.

Edwin Schlossberg: Creating Conversations

Bateson, Gregory. 1972. *Steps to an ecology of mind.* New York: Ballantine Books.

Schlossberg, Edwin. 1970. *Bohr/Stevens letters: Imaginary letters between Neils Bohr and Wallace Stevens.* New York: Institute for the Study of Science in Human Affairs.

————. 1973. *Einstein and Beckett: A record of an imaginary conversation with Albert Einstein and Samuel Beckett.* New York: Links.

————. 1975. *The learning environment for the Brooklyn Children's Museum.* New York: Brooklyn Institute of Arts and Sciences.

Schlossberg, Edwin, and John Brockman. 1975. *The pocket calculator game book.* New York: Morrow.

————. 1977. *The philosopher's game: Match your wits against the 100 greatest thinkers of all time.* New York: St. Martin's Press.

Schlossberg, Edwin, John Brockman, and Lyn Horton. 1978. *The home computer handbook.* New York: Bantam.

5. Considering Context

Kiyoshi Sakashita: Humanware Design

Essential design: Sharp design concept. Unpublished diagram. Sharp Corporation, Osaka. Photocopy.

Evans, Bill. 1990. The Japanese corporate approach. In *Design management: A handbook of issues and methods,* edited by Mark Oakley, 393–405. Cambridge, Mass.: Blackwell Research.

Parkes, Christopher. 1986. Marketing and advertising: Where design is given a high profile. *Financial Times,* 14 August, sec. 1, p. 18.

Powell, Dick. 1982. The human road ahead. *Design* 407 (November): 37–39.

Sakashita, Kiyoshi. Undated. Corporate design for the twenty-first century. *Sharp News.* Photocopy.

Donald Norman: Cognitive Engineering

Gaver, William W. 1994. Grounding social behavior. *Human-Computer Interaction* 9, no. 1: 70–74.

Norman, Donald A. 1988. *The psychology of everyday things.* New York: Basic Books. Reprinted 1990 as *The design of everyday things.* New York: Doubleday.

―――. 1992. *Turn signals are the facial expressions of automobiles.* Reading, Mass.: Addison-Wesley.

―――. 1993. *Things that make us smart: Defending human attributes in the age of the machine.* Reading, Mass.: Addison-Wesley.

―――. 1994. *Defending human attributes in the age of the machine.* Irvington, N.Y.: Voyager. CD-ROM compilation, including *First person: Donald A. Norman; The psychology of everyday things; Things that make us smart;* and *Turn signals are the facial expressions of automobiles.*

Norman, Donald A., and Stephen W. Draper, eds. 1986. *User-centered system design: New perspectives on human-computer interaction.* Hillsdale, N.J.: Lawrence Erlbaum Associates.

John Seely Brown: User-Centering Design

Brown, John Seely. 1991. Research that reinvents the corporation. *Harvard Business Review* 69, no. 1 (January–February): 102–17.

Brown, John Seely, and Paul Duguid. 1992. Enacting design for the workplace. In *Usability: Turning technologies into tools,* edited by Paul S. Adler and Terry A. Winograd, 164–97. New York: Oxford University Press.

―――. 1993. Rethinking the border in design: An exploration of central and peripheral relations in practice. In *The edge of the millennium: An international critique of architecture, urban planning, product and communication design,* edited by Susan Yelavich, 174–89. New York: Whitney Library of Design.

―――. 1994. Borderline issues: Social and material aspects of design. *Human-Computer Interaction* 9, no. 1: 3–36.

Brown, John Seely, Allan Collins, and Paul Duguid. 1989. Situated cognition and the culture of learning. *Educational Researcher* 18, no. 1: 32–42.

Schön, Donald A. 1983. *The reflective practitioner: How professionals think in action.* New York: Basic Books.

―――. 1987. *Educating the reflective practitioner: Toward a new design for teaching and learning in the professions.* San Francisco: Jossey-Bass.

Ubiquitous computing. 1993. N.p.: Xerox Corporation.

Weiser, Mark. 1991. The computer for the 21st century. *Scientific American* 265, no. 3 (September 1): 94–95, 98–102, 104.

6. Thinking Strategically

John Thackara: Cultural Engineering

Interactive Media. 1995. *ID* 42, no. 4 (July–August): 97.

Glancey, Jonathan. 1991. New labels for the designer of desires. *The Independent* (29 June): 36.

Thackara, John. 1993. Consumption and creativity in the information age. In *The edge of the millennium: An international critique of architecture, urban planning, product and communication design,* edited by Susan Yelavich, 160–67. New York: Whitney Library of Design.

Thackara, John, ed. 1986. *New British design.* London: Thames and Hudson.

———. 1988. *Design after modernism: Beyond the object.* London: Thames and Hudson.

van Riet, Kristie, and Willem Velthoven with John Thackara. 1994. *Doors of perception 1* [CD-ROM]. Amsterdam: Mediamatic Interactive Publishing.

Larry Keeley: Strategic Design Planning

Brown, M. Gordon. 1995. The gulf between business and design. *Progressive Architecture* 76, no. 8 (August): 49–50.

Keeley, Larry. 1992. The strategic palette. *Communication Arts* 34, no. 2 (May–June): 134–39.

Pearlman, Chee. 1991. Chicago design planning. *ID* 38, no. 1 (January–February): 34–35.

Robinson, Rick E. 1993. What to do with a human factor: A manifesto of sorts. *American Center for Design Journal* 7, no. 1: 63–73.

Peter Schwartz: Scenario Planning

Brand, Stewart. 1987. *The media lab: Inventing the future at MIT.* New York: Viking.

———. 1994. *How buildings learn: What happens after they're built.* New York: Viking Penguin.

Brown, Tom. 1991. Peter Schwartz: The "art" of taking the long view. *Industry Week* 240, no. 22 (18 November): 12–22.

Hawken, Paul, James Ogilvy, and Peter Schwartz. 1982. *Seven tomorrows: Toward a voluntary history.* New York: Bantam Books.

Schwartz, Peter. 1991. *The art of the long view: Planning for the future in an uncertain world.* New York: Doubleday Currency.

7. Re-viewing Design

John Chris Jones: Of All So Many of Us

Cage, John. 1961. *Silence.* Middletown, Conn.: Wesleyan University Press.

Davies, W. H. 1965. *Complete Poems.* Middletown, Conn.: Wesleyan University Press.

Jones, John Chris. 1978. *Writings remembered.* London: By the author.

———. 1984. *technology changes.* London: Princelet Editions.

———. 1990. depending on everyone: some thoughts on contextual design. *Design Studies* 11, no. 4: 187–93.

———. 1991. *designing designing.* London: ADT Press.

———. 1992. *Design methods.* 2d ed. New York: Van Nostrand Reinhold.

———. 1994. *From the imposed to the adaptive.* Antwerp: Verhaert.

Jones, J[ohn] Christopher, and D. G. Thornley, eds. 1963. *Conference on Design Methods: Papers.* Oxford: Pergamon Press.

Kostelanetz, Richard, ed. 1993. *John Cage: Writer.* New York: Limelight Editions.

Index

The reference, cp (color plate), shown in italic type, refers to illustrations in the photographic insert.